CAN EFFECTIVE SCHOOLS BE INCLUSIVE SCHOOLS?

Institute of Education
UNIVERSITY OF LONDON

Can effective schools be inclusive schools?

**INGRID LUNT AND
BRAHM NORWICH**

First published in 1999 by the
Institute of Education University of London,
20 Bedford Way, London WC1H 0AL
Tel: 020 7612 6000. Fax: 020 7612 6126

Pursuing Excellence in Education

© Institute of Education University of London 1999

British Library Cataloguing in Publication Data:
a catalogue record for this publication is available
from the British Library

ISBN 0 85473 588 7

Produced in Great Britain by
Reprographic Services
Institute of Education University of London

Printed by Formara Limited
16 The Candlemakers, Temple Farm Industrial
Estate, Southend on Sea, Essex SS2 5RX

I1/0006-PEP No6-1099

CONTENTS

FOREWORD

This sixth publication in the Perspectives on Education Policy series, written by Ingrid Lunt and Brahm Norwich, explores whether effective schools can be inclusive schools.

This may seem a straightforward question, but the authors demonstrate that it is not. Effective schools can be inclusive for some groups, while excluding others. Inclusive schools can be effective by some definitions and not others. But this monograph goes well beyond conceptual clarification. It recognises the dilemmas facing real schools and its analysis of DfEE data – on GCSE results and indicators of special educational needs – shows that there are rather few schools that are both effective and inclusive in terms of the criteria most often cited by policymakers.

Some might regard this as an inevitable consequence of policies adopted by British governments in recent years. Unlike some writers in this field, the present authors do not adopt a strong ideological line. Instead they show that policymakers face hard decisions, that well-intentioned policies can have unintended consequences and that we have to make value decisions about what is most important in education.

The authors demonstrate the huge challenge facing schools that seek to be effective and inclusive on a wide range of measures. They do not conclude that such a goal is unrealizable, but they do demonstrate the complexity and magnitude of what it means and entails.

PROFESSOR GEOFF WHITTY
Dean of Research, Institute of Education

September 1999

1
Introduction

SETTING THE CONTEXT

In this introduction we will summarize the development of provision for pupils with special educational needs (SEN) over the past 20 years and consider how the question posed by the title may be addressed in the current policy context. This period has seen enormous changes in policy and provision for pupils with special educational needs. The social and political context which gave rise to the Warnock Report of 1978 and resultant legislation (the 1981 Education Act) has changed from one of equal opportunities and social welfarism to one of individualism and a quasi-market in education. The period 1978-1998 has seen considerable legislative change in education, which has profoundly affected the ways in which LEAs and schools make provision for the diversity of pupils' needs.

We will focus on the period following the Warnock Report (DES, 1978). Special education in this country was dramatically changed by this Report, which provided the foundation for the 1981 Act, the 'integration legislation' of England and Wales. The Report and subsequent legislation paralleled developments in other developed countries, the majority of which passed some form of 'integration' legislation at this time, responding to more general moves towards human rights and equal opportunities.

Before this, provision for pupils, referred to at the time as 'handicapped' in this country, followed a pattern similar to that in other countries. 'Handicapped' pupils were categorized according to disability under one of the 11 categories of handicap provided under the 1944 Act, and provision was usually made in segregated special schools. The most severely handicapped pupils were until the 1970 Education (Handicapped Children) Act deemed ineducable, and were the responsibility of the health rather than the education service. A predominantly medical approach informed the work not only of medical personnel at the time, but also of educational psychologists and other professionals involved in the identification and remediation of pupils' handicaps, whose approach was strongly informed by a medical or 'individual deficit' model of disability.

The Warnock Report provided a major reconceptualization of the nature of special educational needs, and laid the foundations for subsequent developments in policy and provision for these pupils. It provided a strong impetus for integration and for LEAs to develop systems of support for pupils with SEN. Ten years later, the 1988 Education Act threatened to undermine some of these efforts with the introduction of various measures. These included local management of schools and delegation of resources, open enrolment, parental choice and competition between schools, and the pressures and constraints of the National Curriculum and its assessment arrangements. A decade after this, the government paper *Meeting Special Educational Needs. A Programme of Action* (DfEE, 1998) sets out objectives and targets following from the major review of special needs provided by the government Green Paper *Excellence for All Children* (DfEE, 1997), which aim to create more inclusive schools, though with certain provisos. Thus the past 20 years have seen major changes in the way in which pupils' special needs are conceptualized and met, and the attitudes, values and discourse of schools and LEAs.

WARNOCK REPORT 1978

The Warnock Report was produced at a time of widespread concern with civil rights, equal opportunities, human rights and the beginnings of the disability movement. It has come to be regarded as a 'major reformulation' (Wedell, 1990) of ideas of special educational needs and of the kind of provision to be made for pupils with SEN. As is well known, the Report introduced the concept of 'special educational needs', to refer to a wider group of pupils than those previously labelled as handicapped and attending special schools, suggesting that up to one in five pupils might at some time in their school career have special educational needs. The Report emphasized a continuum of special educational needs, with no dividing line between the 'handicapped' and the 'non-handicapped', with pupils' needs changing over time, and as a result of their experience and interaction with the environment. Special educational needs were not to be considered absolute, and only within the child, but were to be thought of as relative to the constraints of the environment, and as a result of an interaction between characteristics of the child and those of the environment, a major aspect of which was the school and its teaching and learning.

The Warnock Report began the move to integration of pupils with SEN into mainstream schools, stating that 'the aims of education are the same for all children' and that children should be integrated where possible. A distinction was made between different forms or degrees of integration; locational (pupils in the same place), social (pupils sharing social time such as lunch time) and functional (pupils sharing teaching and curricula), which could also be seen as a continuum of integration, and has a bearing on a definition of 'inclusive schools'.

It introduced the notion of stages of assessment, stating that assessment of pupils' needs should be continuous and over time (rather than a one-off procedure), and that needs should be identified early; these stages of assessment involved progressively more professionals, according to the complexity of needs. Finally, those children who were deemed in need of a formal record of their SEN would have a statement of special educational needs, as a form of protection, and in recognition of their long-term, severe and complex needs. The statement was intended only for the tiny minority, those who would previously have been placed in a special school, and who now would have the opportunity for integration in mainstream schools with appropriate support. These considerations led to the now somewhat over-used figures: the 2 per cent (those previously in special schools and who might need a statement), the 18 per cent (those with special educational needs in mainstream schools, previously referred to as 'remedial', e.g. Gipps et al, 1987) and the 20 per cent mentioned by the Report (the approximate number of pupils who might experience difficulties in learning at some stage in their school career).

1981 EDUCATION ACT

The Warnock Report provided the foundation for the 1981 Education Act, implemented in 1983. 'The 1981 Act has been widely acclaimed by many educationalists as a progressive and enlightened piece of legislation which has established the field of special educational needs as an important aspect of education' (Norwich, 1992). As is well known, the 1981 Act provided the following definition, which has been retained by subsequent legislation in the 1993 and 1996 Acts:

'A child has special educational needs if he has a learning difficulty which calls for special educational provision to be made for him' and 'a child has a learning difficulty if he has significantly greater difficulty in learning than the majority of children of the same age'.

(Education Act, 1996, Section 312)

The Act required that a child's needs be met in mainstream school, with certain provisos: the efficient use of resources, the provision of efficient education for the children with whom he will be educated and the child's receiving the special educational provision that he requires. This promotes a qualified move to integration, an approach which is maintained by current policy guidelines, and is in line with a commitment to parental choice. Following the 1981 Act, pupils who were considered to have special educational needs and to be in need of additional support beyond that available in the school were put forward for formal assessment and consideration for a statement of special educational need.

LEAs developed a range of services to develop a continuum of provision to meet the range of pupils' SEN (Goacher et al, 1988). For a five-year period, there was a substantial expansion in support services, tutorial units, special classes, specialist teachers and educational psychologists intended to enhance the ability of mainstream schools to meet pupils' needs. LEAs were encouraged to develop a 'continuum of provision' to meet a 'continuum of need' (Fish, 1985). In 1983 the government allocated a significant amount of resources to support in-service training for staff to meet special needs in mainstream schools. This led to the development of one term courses such as the highly successful 'OTIS' courses provided by the London University Institute of Education (Cowne and Norwich, 1987) and in other university centres.

5

With its wider definition of special educational needs, the 1981 Act resulted in a large number of pupils being identified and supported. The notional figure of the Warnock 20 per cent led to an assumption that about 20 per cent of pupils in a class or a school should be identified. It could also be assumed that their needs were somehow different from the needs of others in the class or school, and that they might need specialist or at least different provision. The relative and interactive conceptualization of special educational needs provided by the Act proved, even at the time, very difficult to operationalize (see Goacher et al, 1988; Audit Commission/HMI, 1992). The result was that schools took for granted that they could not be expected to meet the needs of all children. This lack of clarity over definitions of and approaches to special educational needs persists to the present time (Audit Commission/HMI, 1992; Audit Commission, 1998).

In 1992, the HMI and Audit Commission produced a report on *SEN, Getting in on the Act*, which raised fundamental questions about the effectiveness of the 1981 Act in the more competitive climate created by more recent legislation. A major difficulty identified was the lack of clarity over the definition of SEN, which had led to pressure from parents and schools for statements. 'In most schools and LEAs there is no working definition of "special educational need" (Vevers, 1992) and no indication of the level of need which should trigger additional help or resources; this led at the time to a range of proportion of pupils with statements of 0.8 per cent to 3.3 per cent of LEA pupils' population. Increasingly statements were perceived as the way to obtain additional resources, rather than to identify and protect the severe and complex needs of a tiny minority of pupils. Since the 1981 Act there have been three major pieces of legislation (1988, 1993, 1996 Acts) affecting pupils with SEN. None has succeeded in addressing fundamentally the difficulties inherent in the 1981 Act.

Thus, following the 1981 Act, more pupils were identified with special educational needs, both formally with a statement and informally with a label. More pupils in mainstream schools had statements, more pupils in mainstream schools received support from LEA support services, and there was a very slow move towards greater integration of pupils from special schools into mainstream schools (Norwich, 1994, 1997; Swann, 1985, 1988, 1992). Pupils' additional needs were supported by resources from a) a statement, b) LEA support services, or c) support within schools. With the greater financial transparency, pressures and accountability introduced by the 1988 Act, this lack of clarity over the provision of and responsibility for additional resources became a source of even greater concern.

THE 1988 EDUCATION ACT

The 1988 Education Act, claimed to be 'arguably the most important and far-reaching piece of educational law-making since 1944' (Maclure, 1988), introduced fundamental changes to the education system. These had substantial effects on provision for pupils with SEN. Through the introduction of the National Curriculum and assessment arrangements, local management of schools, open enrolment and opting out, the Government introduced competition and market principles into the education system.

Local management of schools and financial delegation had the effect of increasing the demands made on schools to support pupils from within their own budgets at the same time as LEA support services were being reduced. This made even more stark the difficulty of determining who was responsible for providing the resources for pupils with additional educational needs. It emphasized the lack of clarity of definition referred to above, and the absence of clear and consistent criteria for which children should have a statement of SEN. 'This lack of clarity has several consequences. Firstly parents are unclear when they are entitled to extra help for their child. Secondly the respective roles of schools and LEAs have not been defined, leaving room for conflict over who is responsible in any given case. Thirdly, LEAs have an open-ended commitment to an ill-defined group at a time when their resources are limited' (Vevers, 1992:89).

This merely highlighted the difficulty of making decisions about who deserves additional resources when priorities are contentious, resources are finite, demands are infinite and knowledge is partial (Pumfrey, 1996). Decisions of how to share scarce resources, how to prioritize and ration imply fundamental decisions, beliefs and values, whether this be in the education, health or other public welfare system.

THE CONTEXT OF THE 1990s

Since the passing of the 1988 Act, government circulars have demanded progressively greater financial delegation to schools, with the result that LEA support services have been severely reduced. This reduction in LEA support, combined with the pressures of the National Curriculum and the league tables ranking schools for their exam results, means that pupils with SEN may not be welcomed to schools (Evans and Lunt, 1994). The assumption underlying the extensive delegation of budgets to schools is that responsibility for a wider group of pupils is also delegated to schools. Schools are required to make provision out of their delegated budgets for all pupils except the very small minority with severe and complex needs who need a statement. This need for increasing inclusiveness may be considered to sit uneasily with the call for higher standards and increased effectiveness, at least as measured through test and examination results.

Legislation and government policy of the 1990s has sharpened the quasi-market in the education system (Evans and Lunt, 1994), and the introduction of league tables and pressures to raise standards have meant that pupils with special educational needs may not be welcomed to schools (Evans and Lunt, 1994). The assumption of extensive delegation of budgets to schools is that responsibility for a wider group of pupils is also delegated to schools. Schools are required to make provision out of their delegated budgets for all pupils except the very small minority with severe and complex needs who need a statement. This need for increasing inclusiveness may be considered to sit uneasily with the call for higher standards and increased effectiveness, at least as measured through test and examination results.

The 1993 Act and the 1996 Acts did not resolve a fundamental difficulty of the 1981 Act, the unclear definition of special educational needs, and therefore the question which pupils need additional resources. Although the Warnock Report and the 1981 Act abolished categories of handicap, and moved thinking on from a within-child and individual deficit model of disability, to a recognition of the contribution of the teaching and learning environment, there is still no agreement on the questions: what is special about special educational needs, or whether additional needs, individual needs, or specialist needs might be more appropriate concepts and terms for the 1990s. Legislation and government policy in the 1990s have sharpened the quasi-market in the education system (Evans and Lunt, 1994). The introduction of league tables and pressures to raise standards have meant that schools may not consider themselves able to afford to take in pupils with special educational needs, and may find it convenient to continue to use a definition which excludes a certain proportion of pupils, and which attributes to them needs for specialist provision and resources.

We have started by setting the question of whether effective schools can be inclusive schools within the policy context. We will now move on to an analysis of current concepts of effective schooling in section 2, drawing on the positions of proponents of school effectiveness and some of the main critiques of what underlies attributions of effectiveness to schools. One of the key arguments has been that effectiveness has not been relevant to the full diversity of pupils and schools, which leads us into section 3 in which we examine current concepts of inclusive schooling. In setting out the position that inclusiveness is a complex concept and value, we are led to consider in section 4 the question of whether there are limits to school inclusion in principle and in practice. In section 5 we switch from policy and conceptual analysis to examining empirically the question of whether schools having more pupils with SEN have lower attainment levels in the league tables. To do this we draw on DfEE provided data on GCSE school attainment levels for 1998. The book concludes with a summary of the key points in a final section.

2
Concepts of effective schooling

INTRODUCTION

Development in the field of school effectiveness has been presented as progressive, especially by its proponents and practitioners. Its origins are associated with combatting a contemporary pessimism about the impact and potential of schooling in the 1960s and 70s (Mortimore, 1995). However, this is not the view of the current school effectiveness field held by many of its critics (White and Barber, 1997; Slee, Weiner and Tomlinson, 1998). Nevertheless, it is widely recognized that it has a high profile internationally and that it has had an impact on school policy and practice in this country. There has been political interest in the field by politicians who have drawn on its ideas and methods to support political agendas aiming to raise educational standards. This is reflected in the establishment of a School Effectiveness Division within the Government Department for Education and Employment. What is interesting about the school effectiveness movement is its presentation. On one hand, it is portrayed as a young struggling field which needs to tread carefully and with humility. On the other hand it is promoted in an up-beat and almost missionary tone as having great potential to transform and improve schooling (Reynolds, 1998). That it has become something of a bandwagon (Goldstein and Myers, 1997), is not surprising, however, in an international political context in which education and training have become a central political agenda in support of increasingly knowledge-based economies.

SCHOOL EFFECTIVENESS FIELD AND RESEARCH

School effectiveness research has aimed to identify whether different resources, processes and organizational arrangements affect pupil and student outcomes. Its development has centred on the question of why some children in similar catchment areas and learning characteristics are able to produce greater progress than others. School effectiveness research tried to answer this in terms of empirically identified school characteristics. Such characteristics then become the basis for interventions to improve schools. Lauder, Jamieson and Wikeley (1998) refer to this dominant model of school effectiveness as the Received Model (RM). By RM they are referring to the tradition of research associated with Rutter, Power, Reynolds and Mortimore in this country and with Edmonds and Brookover in the USA.

The RM of school effectiveness according to this analysis represents a set of core theoretical assumptions that schools as organizations can have an effect on student or pupil outcomes. This contrasts with the assumption that it is teachers or non-school factors which have effects. Following from this, it is assumed that because of these school effects improvements can be engineered. The RM also assumes that schools are nested organizations within local government and other super-ordinate systems, on one hand, and nest small sub-systems like departments within themselves, on the other. However, schools are also assumed to a have a degree of relative autonomy which makes it possible for them to generate effects independently of super-ordinate factors.

Proponents of the methods associated with the RM of school effectiveness recognize that effectiveness requires a selection of competing educational values (Stoll and Mortimore, 1997), but little more is said than that different value approaches can be combined (p. 10). The tendency is to avoid and even criticize the values debate as preventing what is judged to really count, the focus on effective means (Reynolds, 1998). This is evident also in the definition of an effective school as:

> 'one in which pupils progress further than might be expected from consideration of its intake' (Stoll and Mortimore, 1997:10).

This focus on attributing differential progress between schools to school characteristics and processes reveals a primary interest in teasing out school input from student entry factors. An alternative definition of school effectiveness also shows that the RM is about the capability of the school to make a difference:

> 'an effective school regularly promotes the highest academic and other achievement for the maximum of its students, regardless of the socio-economic backgrounds of their families' (Mortimore, quoted in Mortimore and Sammons, 1997).

This definition differs from the previous one in only making reference to socio-economic background rather than the more general intake, which can include student baseline learning characteristics. It also makes mention of promoting the 'highest academic standards or other achievements'. This implies that there is an implicit goal to maximize learning progress rather than attain adequate progress. This could be taken to mean that effective schools are the highest attaining ones given their intake. It is not clear whether schools which promote progress, but not the highest levels of progress, can be counted as effective. This point might not matter in research work, but it is of crucial relevance when these concepts are applied to the diversity of real schools. It is not clear whether the effectiveness of a school is a categorical, yes or no, matter or a continuum. If it is a continuum it would be useful to know how to apply the concept of effectiveness to the diversity of schools.

Another feature of the above definition is that it makes reference to promoting achievement for the maximum of students. This resembles the utilitarian notion of maximizing happiness for the maximum number of people. It is an important part of any definition of school effectiveness because it takes account of effectiveness for whom. As school effectiveness theorists now realize, 'effectiveness' has to be considered in terms of effectiveness for which outcomes, over what period of time and for whom (Mortimore and Sammons, 1997). It is clear that in relation to the question of effective for whom, that effective for the maximum students is more inclusive or egalitarian than effective for the minority of very able high attainers. However, effective for the maximum is not the same as effective for all, for the full diversity of students and pupils. So, we have here in the very definition of school effectiveness the assumption that a minority, whatever its size, which we can assume to be those with special educational needs, will not be counted in identifying school effectiveness. This is a critical point for the argument in this paper which considers whether an effective school can be an inclusive one. We will return to it later in this section and again towards the end of the paper.

The focus in school effectiveness on the capability of the school to promote learning outcomes leads to the search for methods of estimating the contribution of schools to student progress. This is where the concept of value added was introduced with techniques to assess the average progress for a school. It is claimed that schools can be compared in terms of their effectiveness by adjusting achievements for various background factors, such as the number of pupils eligible for free school meals, and for prior attainment. The significance of the value added concept is that it distances the concept of school effectiveness from the concept of high attaining schools. This is a very important point as school effective researchers have been keen to point out that league tables of schools' average academic results are not a fair way of evaluating their relative capabilities of promoting learning progress. The promise of value added analyses has been that schools with intakes of students from low socio-economic backgrounds can demonstrate similar and even higher levels of value added than schools having students from more advantaged backgrounds. However, although policy makers now recognize the force of this argument, there are continuing technical issues in estimating value added measures for schools (Goldstein and Thomas, 1995).

CRITIQUES OF SCHOOL EFFECTIVENESS

Criticisms of the field come from different quarters. Some come from within the field by those who hold some of the basic assumptions of what has been called the Received Model. Others come from theorists interested in educational organizations and management but who have reservations about the RM. Still other critiques come from policy makers who question the value of educational research, while further criticisms come from academic theorists who question the very basis of the RM and the epistemological and research assumptions used in it.

The prominence of school effectiveness has been attributed to the relationship between policy-makers and school effective researchers in the recent and current educational and political context (Slee and Weiner, 1998). Policy-makers have been pursuing resolutions to what has been seen as a crisis in state education, while school effective researchers have been identifying the characteristics of effective schools which underpin moves to improve schools. It has also been noted that the field appeals to commonsense notions that all schools should be effective and that we would naturally wish to improve schools. This use of everyday terms is deceptive as criticisms of the field can then come to be seen as overly negative. However, it is important to realize that teachers' and parents' non-technical interest in school effectiveness and school improvement does not have to translate only into the assumptions and techniques of the dominant model, the Received Model. This is where Lauder's analysis, discussed above, is so useful. The relative lack of open analysis of this model's assumptions has spurred the critical positions which Lauder calls the Heretical Model (HM). The HM deals more with general criticisms about episte-mological, meta-theoretical and value issues than the specific details which are the bread and butter of the RM. Typical of the HM is the assertion that school effectiveness is about 'peddling feel-good fictions' which are 'technically and morally problematic' (Hamilton, 1996: 54-6). One does not have to be so dismissive of the school effectiveness field as this to realize that some of the weaknesses of the RM can be addressed in other models of effectiveness. This is where Lauder, Jamieson and Wikeley's Contextual Model (CM) offers an example of a positive alternative and potentially useful synthesis. In the CM teacher professional autonomy and the uniqueness of each school as an organization in its social context is acknowledged at the same time as seeking systematic improvement of schools:

> Research with the CM will fundamentally be concerned with the link between capacities, potential and limits within specific positions within an educational market. (Lauder, Jamieson and Wikeley, 1998:63)

The judgement of schools in terms of league tables and value added analyses is rejected in the CM if these do not take account of significant contexts, such as the school's community, its intake and the educational market. The capability of schools to raise academic achievements is also seen in terms of how far such changes can be sustained rather than just occur for a limited time under external pressures.

One of the specific criticisms of the RM of school effectiveness is that some of its proponents can at times and to certain audiences claim too much for the concept and their findings (Goldstein and Myers, 1997, Lauder, Jamieson and Wikley, 1998). The point is that the differences which schools can make are limited and contrast with the rhetoric of promoters. These limitations in turn call into question the authority of the research in guiding school improvement practice. What we find is an interesting mixture of missionary praise for the school effectiveness movement with reminders about the need for humility about the findings and research methods (Grace, 1998).

From within the RM it has been noted that the lessons of the last 20 years of school effectiveness research indicate that the term school effectiveness is a misnomer (Goldstein and Myers, 1997). Effectiveness has been shown to be multi-dimensional in that schools differ in effectiveness by curriculum subject, for different groups of pupils and over time (Gray et al, 1996; Thomas, 1997, Thomas et al, 1998; Mortimore, 1998). This is a very important point for the theme of this paper as it implies that empirically we have no grounds to talk about effective schools as a single continuum. It implies that effectiveness phenomena have to be more carefully identified than is currently the case in the application of school effective ideas and techniques. It therefore becomes more valid to consider the effectiveness of schools in terms of profiles based on schools' capabilities to promote learning in different areas of learning, for different groups of students and for different time periods. It is interesting that this is a degree of complexity which can been identified even within the assumptions of the RM.

That effectiveness is relative to different learning outcomes is connected to the criticism that school effectiveness research has concentrated overly on cognitive and short-term outcomes. There are different perspectives on this. Many school effectiveness researchers (Mortimore, Reynolds, Goldstein) recognize now that a wider range of outcomes needs to be examined. In some research, for example, non-cognitive outcomes have been examined, such as attitudes and self-esteem (the Junior School Project, Mortimore et al, 1988). But, the issue is not that short-term cognitive achievements are unimportant goals, as they are clearly important to many people with a stake in education. The problem arises from the fact that longer term cognitive outcomes and more general affective, social and motivational characteristics are also important for many people. Any unwillingness to engage in the values or goals debate means that the educational effectiveness studies stick with limited and superficially feasible criteria of effectiveness. When challenged, school effectiveness researchers make statements about broadening criteria but have difficulties in doing so. What needs to be addressed are the problems in broadening effectiveness criteria, as the rhetoric of widening criteria is easy but the practice harder. School effectiveness workers need to specify what these wider outcomes are and how to assess them in practice (Grace, 1998).

Were these issues addressed then it would be realized that education is inevitably concerned with multiple and sometimes contrary values and goals. It is not a question of whether schools should have as a goal either self-directing citizenship (White and Barber, 1997:53) or basic academic skills in numeracy or literacy. It is rather a question of the extent to which these and other important goals can be met jointly. This is a question of priority and balance while holding onto several goals, not of splitting and focusing on single outcomes and ignoring others. Effectiveness studies need therefore to examine the relationships between different goals and outcomes. For example, does a focus on short-term cognitive outcomes support positive affective and social outcomes or undermine them? This is also where the criticisms of the reductionist assumptions and the use of quantitative measures in the

RM are relevant. Some critics have noted that these assumptions and methods have reinforced the Government's view that quality in education can be measured by test and pencil and paper measures. This is where Grace's (1998) call for a more catholic approach to school effectiveness is relevant, when he recommends a more innovative conceptual and methodological approach: 'by extending the important concept of "value-added" research to include the equally important concept of "values-added" inquiry' (Grace, 1998:124).

Criticisms of the outcomes used in the RM also relate to epistemological concerns about its positivist and reductionist assumptions. These criticisms are part of a wider and deeper debate about the nature of knowledge and its generation in educational studies and research. Criticisms of positivism in this context are usually associated with a rejection of assumptions that research can be neutral in value terms and support for the assumption that context is important for the meaning and use of theoretical concepts like school effectiveness. Schooling cannot be understood simply in terms of general causal processes as there is a degree of indeterminacy. What is missing in the RM is an interpretivist or hermeneutical dimension to the study of schooling (Scott, 1997). The details of these basic criticisms are not relevant to this section other than to note the links between the values and epistemological issues. Grace (1998) summarizes these when he refers to the *technical reductionism* in the RM version of school effective research. This includes two aspects: *contextual reductionism* which is about the knowledge process of abstracting performance outcomes of schooling from their social and historical context, and *mission reductionism* which is about the abstracting of academic performance indicators from the integrated matrix of school outcomes. The implication of this analysis is that research into school effectiveness needs to be aware of the limitations of different research orientations and does not have to be confined to any one methodological approach.

The relationship between social science and policy research and

Government policy is a complex one in which both parties are dependent on each other but also have distinct and sometimes contrary interests and agendas. This applies to the relationships between school effectiveness researchers and policy-makers, though it is difficult to generalize. There is no one school effectiveness position. Different proponents can and do adopt different positions, some adopt different positions at different times and to different audiences and some even change their positions over time. But critics have pointed out that school effectiveness work has been abused for political purposes and used by policy-makers as a legitimizing device (Goldstein and Myers, 1997). From policy-makers and political perspective, school effectiveness has been seen as having a contribution to make to their agenda of 'raising standards', when it is not necessarily connected to political agendas about standards. A related criticism is that school effectiveness work has been used to justify the policy and practice of blaming schools for 'failing' and that there have been some notable silences about the impact of the National Curriculum, market principles, competition and league tables. It is not surprising that there have been calls for keeping more distance from short term policy demands and the need to adopt longer term and more independent research programmes (Goldstein and Myers, 1997).

SCHOOL EFFECTIVENESS AND CHILDREN WITH SEN

The relationship between the fields of school effectiveness and special education as two distinct areas of educational studies has been a curious one. Pupils with learning difficulties and disabilities were not the prime concern in early studies of school effects. Though school effectiveness studies over the last decade have examined differential effects for different ability or attainment groups, this has still not included those in special schools or even those with significant difficulties in learning in mainstream schools. This has been partly a matter of not seeing these students as part of mainstream educational issues, but underlying this are the practical and technical issues of assessing differential progress in these special needs groups. There have been no comparable studies of special schools effectiveness using the same methods as in typical RM studies. It has, for example, taken ten years for the Government to do something about the exclusion of pupils from the assessment arrangements of the National Curriculum (NC) (QCA, 1998). Over the last year guidance about assessment criteria for pupils working towards level 1 of the NC have been issued. This was only prompted by the requirement that all schools should be engaged in school target setting, an agenda somewhat distant from basic curriculum and assessment needs for pupils with SEN.

However, to some interested in special education, school effectiveness research with its focus on environmental factors in the form of school processes and characteristics, provided a welcome alternative to and mode of resisting individual deficit models of difficulties in learning. For some theorists, improving schools would have benefits for pupils with SEN (Ramasut and Reynolds, 1993, Stoll, 1991). The focus on schools as organizations had a definite appeal to those interested in the education of pupils with SEN in mainstream schools. It switched the locus from the individual, from what was called 'within-child' factors to school and teaching ones. This meant that when pupils experienced difficulties in learning, this could be taken as calling for reform of the school and teaching rather than changing their deficit. Ainscow (1991) used this school and teaching focus as a way of denying that difficulties in learning could have an individual basis. Special educational needs in this perspective came to be seen as a way of individualizing and stigmatizing pupils, rather than as an indicator of the need to make schools more effective for all:

In attempting to conceptualise educational difficulty in a more positive way we can more usefully see pupils experiencing difficulty as indicators of the need for reform. They point to the need to improve schooling in ways that will enable them to achieve success … It is worth adding at this stage that I believe that such reforms would be to the benefit of all pupils. Consequently, the aim is *effective schools for all.* (Ainscow, 1991:3, author's own italics)

This switch of focus on to changes within mainstream schools came at a time when policy and legislation was promoting the education of pupils with SEN in mainstream schools. This was in tune with current ideas for whole school SEN policies and the development of internal school practices of learning support. However, this coming together of school effectiveness and improvement ideas and special education interests has proved to be more short-term and superficial than it appeared at the time. As some of the original enthusiasts came to realize (Reynolds, 1995; Slee, 1998), there were some basic differences between school effectiveness and special education interests over value and focus issues. The RM of school effectiveness work has not taken up the notion of effective schools for all. This is because most of the RM concepts of effectiveness, as discussed above, focus on the capability of promoting learning for the majority of pupils. On the other hand, those promoting effective schools for all have assumed that school and teaching changes geared for those with difficulties in learning and disabilities will benefit those without difficulties. This has been an assumption and even acted as a rallying call, but not one which has been examined intensively either conceptually or in terms of empirical evidence. Are schools which maximize outcomes for a minority with difficulties and disabilities also those that maximize for the majority? This question will be examined in a later section.

3
Concepts of inclusive schooling

The idea of inclusion in education came to be used in the context of a concern to educate pupils and students with disabilities and difficulties in learning in mainstream settings. As we discuss in this section, the term has come to take on a wider significance and popularity in linking up with the recent development of the concept of inclusion or social inclusion as a broader social and political value. Inclusion in this wider sense is comparable to equality as a social value in relating to all aspects of social disadvantage, oppression and discrimination. Social inclusion was developed as an alternative political conception and value to counter the dominance of market values in the 1980s and early 1990s.

CURRENT CONCEPTS

With the growth of interest in inclusive education there has been a wide range of perspectives about inclusion. Some are presented as part of policy documents and positions, while other perspectives are set out by academic and professional commentators. In this section we start by outlining some recent policy perspectives.

In the recent DfEE Programme of Action – Meeting SEN (DfEE, 1998), inclusion is described as a process, not a fixed state, and involves many different things:

> the placement of pupils with SEN in mainstream schools, the participation of all pupils in the curriculum and social life of mainstream schools, the participation of all pupils in learning which leads to the highest possible level of achievement, and the participation of young people in the full range of social experiences and opportunities once they have left school. (DfEE, 1998:23)

The current Government's position on school inclusion is to promote it 'where parents want it and appropriate support can be provided' (page 23, section 1). It is clear that although there has been a strong push to review and renew moves towards greater inclusion, that the basic conceptions have changed little since the previous Conservative Government.

> For some children, a mainstream placement may not be right, or not right just yet. We confirm, therefore that specialist provision – often but not always in special schools – will continue to play a vital role. (DfEE, 1998:23)

This continuity of Government policy can be seen in the principles set out in the SEN Code of Practice, (DfEE, 1994):

> The needs of most pupils will be met in the mainstream and without statutory assessment or a Statement of SEN. Children with SEN, including those with Statements of SEN, should, where appropriate

and taking into account the wishes of their parents, be educated alongside their peers in mainstream schools.

This conditional commitment to inclusion was also evident in the Labour Government's SEN Green Paper (DfEE, 1997), in talking about 'inclusion of children with SEN within mainstream schooling wherever possible'. There is also continuity with the basic conditions set out in legislation from the original formulation in the Education Act 1981. This placed the onus on Local Education Authorities (LEAs) to educate all children in the mainstream, subject to four key conditions: 1. that the child's special needs were being met, 2. that this did not interfere with the education of other children involved, 3. that it be compatible with the 'efficient' use of resources and 4. that it took account of parental wishes. These conditions can be seen to represent the interests of those involved, the child with a disability or difficulty in learning, his or her peers, the parents and the LEA responsible for deciding about special provision. They set the commitment to inclusion as hanging on the relative weighting of these potentially contrary factors. Another feature of the current Government policy is that the onus is for inclusion in mainstream schools not necessarily mainstream classes.

Although the Labour Government's Green Paper expresses support for the UNESCO Salamanca Statement on special educational needs, this UNESCO Statement goes well beyond the conditional Government commitment to inclusion:

- Every child has a fundamental right to education and must be given the opportunity to achieve and maintain an acceptable level of learning;
- Every child has unique characteristics, interests, abilities and learning needs;
- Educational systems should be designed and educational programmes implemented to take account of the wide diversity of these characteristics and needs;
- Those with special educational needs must have access to regular

schools which should accommodate them within a child-centred pedagogy capable of meeting their needs;

- Regular schools with this inclusive orientation are the most effective means of combatting discriminatory attitudes, creating welcoming communities, building an inclusive society and achieving education for all; moreover they provide effective education for the majority of children and improve the efficiency and ultimately the effectiveness of the entire system. (UNESCO, 1994)

It is clear that there are different conceptions about inclusion which have a very significant bearing on the extent and nature of educational provision for students with disabilities and difficulties. Bailey (1998) from an Australian context outlines a definition which would reflect the perspectives of many in this country too: 'Inclusion refers to being in an ordinary school with other students, following the same curriculum at the same time, in the same classrooms, with the full acceptance of all, and in a way which makes the student feel no different from other students' (Bailey, 1998:173).

This definition focuses on three key aspects:

1. physically being in the same place,

2. doing the same as other students,

3. being socially accepted and feeling a sense of belonging.

Inclusion in this sense is usually contrasted with the now less favoured and used term integration, which is seen to reflect physical placement in the mainstream and the expectation that the student assimilates, as it is said, to the unchanged mainstream system. By contrast, in inclusion the mainstream school adapts and restructures to respond to the needs of students (Ainscow, 1995). Whether integration was actually used to imply a lack of school adaptation and response can be doubted, but it is clear that the force of the newer term inclusion is to focus on systemic school adaptation and not just for individuals separately.

However, Booth (1996) has criticized concepts of inclusion and inclusive education which purport to describe an ideal state or aim. He argues that reference to inclusive schools implies that inclusion is an attainable state and that good practice can be identified. Booth believes that there are few examples of inclusive schools which include all children from the neighbourhood, and therefore that it is better to think in terms of inclusion as an 'unending set of processes'. For Booth, inclusion :

> comprises two linked processes: it is the process of increasing the participation of students in the cultures and curricula of mainstream schools and communities; it is the process of reducing exclusion of students from mainstream cultures and communities. (Booth, 1996:96)

This focus on defining inclusion in terms of participation aims to underline the significance of inclusion as something which cannot be done to people, it is something in which people are actively involved. Florian, (1998), for example, argues that the opportunity to participate is quite different from making available conditions of everyday life, associated with normalization.

> Opportunity to participate implies active involvement and choice as opposed to passive receipt of a pattern or condition that has been made available. Locational, social and functional integration are things that are made available. (Florian, 1998:17)

Concepts of inclusion which focus on greater pupil participation in mainstream settings and linked notions of active involvement and by implication choice, contrast with notions of inclusion which relate to schools responding to all pupils:

> Inclusive education describes the process by which a school attempts to respond to all pupils as individuals by reconsidering and

restructuring its curricular organization and provision and allocating resources to enhance equality of opportunity. Through this process, the school builds its capacity to accept all pupils from the local community who wish to attend and, in so doing, reduces the need for exclusion. (Sebba and Sachdev, 1997:9)

If the inclusive school is restructured to accommodate the full diversity of pupils in a community, then such reform of the mainstream schools provides opportunities for and welcomes pupils with disabilities and difficulties in learning. But to be welcomed and accommodated is different from actively wishing to participate in mainstream settings. The difference between these two foci – on restructured mainstream schools and on active participation – shows some of the complexity of the inclusion concept. There is an important distinction between inclusion as a placement in restructured mainstream schools, as an opportunity for participation and as a choice to participate.

Though some theorists consider mainstream placement as a basic, though not sufficient, condition of inclusion, there is an authoritative concept of inclusion which does not even define inclusion in terms of the same location. In the Tomlinson Committee Report on post-school education of those with learning difficulties and disabilities (Tomlinson, 1997), inclusive learning is defined as a system which is inclusive but not necessarily an integrated setting. Tomlinson states that: 'No apology is necessary for the paradox, as some have seen it, that the Committee's concept of inclusive learning is not necessarily coincident with total integration of the students into the 'mainstream' (Tomlinson, 1997:193). He then goes on to explain that :

The Committee was asked to advise how matters could be improved assuming limited resources. Full integration implies a very well resourced education system, if it is to do justice to all the students who would, as a matter of dogma, then always be taught in the same setting. The number of teachers and other experts that would need to be deployed, together with the range of technological help needed, would be more expensive than is now the case, where concentration of resources is achieved. (Tomlinson, 1997:193)

The significance of Tomlinson's concept of inclusion is that participation operates at different levels: the education system as a whole, the institution and the teacher in a particular setting. The right to participate at one level might or might not be matched by participation at another level. Whether it is matched at each level depends on resourcing but also on individual students' learning needs. As Tomlinson goes on: 'Full integration as an aim should be retained, and when achieved, it will be coincident with inclusive learning' (Tomlinson, 1997:193).

LINKS TO WIDER CONCEPTS OF SOCIAL INCLUSION

For many inclusion theorists educational inclusion is part of a wider interest in an inclusive society (Thomas, 1997; Barton, 1997; Booth and Ainscow, 1998). An inclusive philosophy in education is not limited to disability or other vulnerable groups but to all students and pupils. Barton (1997) presents inclusive education as about responding to diversity, empowering all members and celebrating difference. It stems from demands for an inclusive society which stands for 'social justice, equity and democratic participation' (page 233). This is presented as implying a critical stance in which barriers to their realization need to be 'identified, challenged and removed'. For Thomas (1997) the popularity of inclusion in education comes from its links with wider notions of inclusivity and social inclusion. He relates these wider notions of inclusion to the development of social policy ideas around the concepts of stake-holding and the social costs of those not participating in different areas of society. The Labour Government has adopted the term social inclusion and built it into an important part of its social policy, as shown in the establishment of the Social Inclusion Unit to examine relevant areas for policy development. The notion of increasing social inclusion has come to replace previous policy analysis and positions about increasing social and economic equality.

For Booth and Ainscow (1998), inclusion is not only a process connected to exclusion, but applies to all kinds of exclusion, not being limited to students with disabilities and difficulties. In adopting this stance they are attempting to challenge the notion of 'special educational needs' and to redefine the field of educating students with disabilities and difficulties, special education, in terms of the processes of inclusion and exclusion. Booth is aware that in wanting to broaden the focus of inclusion, he is going against positions held within the disability movement that concentrate on inclusion and disability (Oliver, 1992). In supporting his position, he tries to detract from a focus on disability by suggesting that certain groups might not wish to have this term applied to them. Though this may continue to be true for some groups, the term disability has changed over the last decade, and can be broadened beyond physical disability. It is now used in legislation (Disability Discrimination Act) to include a range of wider difficulties. Members of the disability movement have also come to adopt it in its wider sense.

It is important to see the connections and common interests between those with disabilities and difficulties in learning and other groups subject to exclusionary processes in their common experiences of disadvantage and discrimination. But while those from ethnic minorities, gender groups, and smaller groups such as travellers and pregnant teenage girls are subject to similar social processes, this does not detract from disability-specific experiences and conditions. Inclusive education can be defined either to cover the wider range of disadvantaged groups or to be confined to those with disabilities in the wider sense. This is a matter of definition and choice, but it is important that the distinction between the more specific disability and the broader all-encompassing meanings are not blurred and confused. Members of different disadvantaged groups can have distinct identities related to their social and personal conditions even when sometimes they may have multiple identities, such as having a disability, and being a female Bengali. It is also notable that any criticism of disability-specific issues in terms of uncertainties about group range and membership apply even more to the overall group of those subject to exclusionary processes. The tendency to make a dichotomy between specific disadvantaged groups and the overall group defined in terms of the general processes of exclusion and inclusion needs to be resisted.

The attempt to incorporate and even to dissolve a specific disability focus can be seen to reflect a commitment to inclusion as a general social and political value. But this commitment to inclusion is to a super-ordinate, complex and abstract value, like equality or justice. Like these general values inclusion cannot be simply applied to the many areas and contexts of teaching and learning, let alone other areas of social life. This is because like equality, there are different aspects and features of what is meant by inclusion and inclusiveness. Inclusion theorists, like those quoted above, assume that students have a right to be part of the mainstream (1), but also a right to positive evaluation and respect (2). This is evident in their justifications for increasing participation and for reducing exclusion. But, in addition to the right to participate and to respect there is also an implied right to individually relevant learning (3). This emerges, for example, in the value placed on schools being 'responsive to differences between all students' (Booth, Ainscow and Dyson, 1998:224). If inclusive values are considered to underpin these three broad kinds of rights for all, then it becomes clear that inclusion is a complex value over which there will be uncertainties about its applicability. For example, if the right to be part of the mainstream means being in the same location as others (1) and being respected (2), then any separate provision, even in a withdrawal group, could be considered as exclusionary, whether this provides individually relevant learning or not.

THE COMPLEXITY OF EDUCATIONAL INCLUSION

This analysis indicates that there are quite divergent and incompatible concepts of inclusion and that it is a complex concept open to confusion. We have identified these differences and complexities:

1 Bailey's view that it is about learning in the same place on the same curriculum as others.

2 Tomlinson's view that it is not necessarily about being in the same place and curriculum.

3 Booth's and Ainscow's view that it is not a state at all, but an unending process of increasing participation.

4 Thomas's view that it is about accepting all children.

5 Sebba's and Sachdev's view that it is about schools responding and restructuring their provision.

6 Florian's view that opportunity to participate in inclusion is about active involvement and choice and not something done to the disabled.

The position that inclusion is an unending process serves to keep the concept open and protect the ideal; however, not specifying steps towards the inclusive goal makes it hard to apply the term and to identify progress towards inclusion. So, how do we know whether one form of provision is more inclusive than another? How does physical proximity to mainstream activities compare with social acceptance of students with disabilities and difficulties? How important is active involvement in mainstream settings compared with social acceptance? Is greater physical proximity with low social acceptance more inclusive than less physical proximity but greater social acceptance ? What can happen without specifying steps or criteria for a complex value like inclusion is that any educational practice which involves some, but not pure inclusive features, can come to be identified as exclusionary. For example, if a student with a disability or difficulty wishes to have some individual teaching outside her mainstream class separate from her peers, then this system could be dismissed as exclusionary, even when it has many of the features of inclusive practices. Inclusion as an unending process goes with thinking in terms of dichotomies, a kind of purist either-or thinking which can end up condemning any form or degree of separate provision or distinct support system.

In this respect Low (1997) makes an interesting and provocative distinction between different kinds of inclusivists: **hard, soft** and **stupid inclusivists**. In his analysis, **hard inclusivists** believe that all needs should be taken care of as part of general social arrangements. Systems of education should in this view be designed to include the full diversity. **Soft inclusivists** believe in supporting systems which enable maximum independence for those with disabilities and recognize that this requires special support and provision. For them, inclusion is about this provision and support being available as part of mainstream arrangements. **Stupid inclusivists**, according to Low, recognize the need for special provision and support in practice, but do not like to call it 'special'. An example of this would be the avoidance of the word 'special' because this language is seen as 'retarding the development of thinking about inclusion' (Booth, 1996:89). Low considers hard inclusivism wrong in principle and practice, as it denies, in his view, that people with disabilities, although they share common needs with all others, also have distinct and specific needs – what he is willing to call special needs. It is not clear whether Low believes that hard inclusivists turn out in practice to recognize the need for special provision, but do not like to call it special, and are therefore also stupid inclusivists. However, it is probably only someone like Low who has a disability of sight who is in a position to use such a provocative typology of inclusivists.

4
Are there limits to school inclusion in principle and practice?

Despite contemporary interest in developing effective schools, there is complexity and some confusion in key ideas about improving schools and making them more effective. As we discussed in the last section, those who advocate effective schools for all assume that what is effective for the minority is effective for the majority (Ainscow,1991, 1995). But, as Reynolds (1995) in this country and Gerber (1996) in the USA have argued, schools and practices which are associated with high attainments for students with disabilities and difficulties are not necessarily associated with high attainments for the modal or average student. Gerber explains that there is an often overlooked conflict between public education geared to universal education and special education, which comes from: 'the insistence that design and deployment of instructional effort within schools could and should be modified to accommodate individual differences rather than expectations for modal students' (Gerber, 1996:170).

Applied to the current context in this country, this leads us to ask whether what is commonly called an effective school can be an inclusive one. The answer depends on what counts as effective and as inclusive. One option is to define effective in terms of inclusive values and say that for a school to be effective it has to include the diversity of pupils. This is what many within special education advocate, but to do so defines effective in terms of process criteria, not in terms of optimizing learning outcomes as is done in the RM of school effectiveness. For example, Corbett (1999) argues that for a school to be called effective it should demonstrate strategies to protect, nurture and encourage its most vulnerable members. However, such calls for criteria of effectiveness in terms of celebrating difference can be seen as critical counters that wish away the dominant conceptions, rather than relate conceptually to these models. As we argued in the last section, the current definitions of effectiveness either make no reference to the range or diversity of pupils or refer to the maximum, explicitly not including the minority. The methods of research also assume that it is the modal not the exceptional pupil who is the focus of interest. Schools are not identified as effective when their lowest attaining pupils show significant attainment gains. This is also demonstrated in Government target setting policies for raising standards. So, if the effective or successful school is the one with consistently high A-C GCSE or level 4 literacy and numeracy results, then this excludes a significant minority with lower attainments from the operational concept of effectiveness.

Another option is to define effective schooling in the dual terms of intake and outcomes. In intake terms schools would be more effective, the more open access there is to the diversity of pupils in a community. In outcome terms, schools would also be more effective the more they maximize the learning outcomes of all pupils, not just the majority. To adopt a more complex notion of effectiveness we need to be clear that we are dealing with two elements, first, including pupil diversity and second, maximizing outcomes, both of which are themselves complex notions. As discussed in a previous section, there is in addition the question of which outcomes are maximized and whether once we adopt multiple outcomes, if maximizing some outcomes goes with maximizing other outcomes. There is also the question of whether maximizing any outcome just means optimizing the average outcome level or whether it means optimizing the mean and reducing the variation between the highest and lowest outcomes. This is the question about whether in seeking effectiveness we are seeking maximum outcomes or just satisfactory levels. In this section we examine what including diversity means and whether there are limits to inclusion.

MULTIPLE VALUES AND POLICY AND PLANNING DILEMMAS ABOUT DIFFERENCE

The problems that emerge in the planning of education provision and setting of learning standards in a genuinely inclusive way are those that have arisen historically in the continuing uncertainties about equality as a guiding educational value amongst other educational values. They are problems that do not disappear in the new language about social inclusion. They can be posed in these terms. Do we set standards in terms of attainment levels largely irrespective of individual differences in pupils' starting levels and available material and human resources for learning ? If we do, as the current government has for literacy and numeracy at key stage 2, then we have to consider the relevance of these standards for 'exceptional' pupils who are distant from the modal standard.

As a second option, we could abandon a concept of equality defined in terms of the same or minimum outcome levels for all, if we take account of starting individual differences. We could then interpret equality in terms of similar gains from different starting levels. This would mean legitimizing different starting levels and outcomes, which some might see as undermining a commitment to equality. There would also be technical assessment questions about valid comparisons of gains for pupils across different attainment levels. It might also mean that additional instructional resources would have to be applied to lower attainers to achieve learning gains similar to the higher attainers.

In a third option we could abandon common standards for all, whether these are defined in terms of the same outcomes or gains. In one version there would be no common standards at all, only standards set individually. This could present major practical problems of individualizing, but more important, it would mean relinquishing any prospect of interpreting equality in terms of comparability to general standards. In another version of this third option, different standards would be acknowledged for different groups (identified in attainment or social background terms). The aim would be to reduce the differences between these standards. This option retains common standards in the form of reducing attainment differences. It gives up equality in its simple interpretation in the first two options and replaces it with the value of reducing inequalities. But, there still remain questions about how to decide which standards are relevant to which individuals and groups. This move from options 1 and 2 to option 3 represents what Walzer (1983) has advocated in moving from what he calls 'simple equality' to 'complex equality'. In simple equality everyone gets access to the same thing, whereas in complex equality distribution varies according to different criteria. Ideas of complex equality are relevant to the contemporary interest in differences and what has come to be called the politics of difference. But, as Walzer recognizes, this leaves us to decide what is a 'relevant difference' for different treatments, which is another way of putting the problem associated with the third option 3, just discussed.

One of the basic reasons for the problems and uncertainties about inclusion in education is that we do not have simple and single ideas and values about educational excellence. As with equality, we cannot avoid complex ideas about inclusion. This arises in part from contradictions or dilemmas about educational values themselves and in part from practical limitations in our current capabilities to resolve problems in education and the wider society. These dilemmas arise from multiple values which cannot be assumed to be mutually compatible in full, leaving us to have to make difficult decisions that involve balancing and trade-offs.

This can be illustrated, as we have explained above, by the way in which inclusion theorists take students to have a right to participate in the mainstream, but also to have a right to respect and acceptance. In addition it is widely assumed that students have a right to individually relevant learning. Other rights are also invoked, such as, to have some choice about the institution of learning and to achieve a basic minimum either in terms of outcomes or genuine opportunity. Conceptual analysis shows that not all these rights or entitlements are fully compatible with each other. For instance, if rights are extended to some, then they apply to all. This means that there is the continuing risk that minorities, such as those with disabilities and difficulties, are subject to majority interests, which do not necessarily take the interests of the disabled, let alone their rights, into account. An incompatibility of rights can arise from the potential tension between the minority's right to participate in the mainstream and the majority's right to individually relevant learning and choice about the institution of learning. Unless some rights are given priority over others and backed by legislative systems, minorities are prone to the dominance and exclusion by the majority. There can also be a tension between the right of parents of pupils with disabilities and difficulties (and sometimes pupils themselves) to choose a separate institution of learning when a majority of parents of pupils with disabilities choose to participate in mainstream institutions.

It should not be surprising that there can be clashes between different rights and entitlements, as one person's or agency's entitlement places a potential requirement or constraint on another person or agency. Rights and entitlement require the provision of resources and others' acceptance or tolerance of compliance. The implications are that we take seriously the multiple nature of values and associated rights or entitlements in the educational field and that we understand the implicit social conflicts and interrelationships between mass school education and 'special' education. Much is heard about conflicts and contradictions from critical perspectives on special education. These aim to reveal oppression and unmask concealed dominant interests in current and historical policy and practice. However, it has been argued recently that these critical perspectives assume values and principles without detailed conceptual and empirical grounding (Clark, Dyson and Millward, 1998). They interpret policy and practice in terms of idealized models and ideal types of provision, rather than in terms of more complex ideals and the range of experienced realities. Little is also heard about any tensions within individuals and agencies when they aim to increase participation in mainstream settings, while they also aim to increase teaching and learning opportunities for those with disabilities and difficulties. These tensions represent dilemmas between providing optimally for individual learning needs and for participation and acceptance in the mainstream. These dilemmas which have been called *dilemmas of difference*, take the form that if you include and treat those with disabilities and difficulties in the same ways as most others, individually relevant learning opportunities could be denied; but, if you treat them in individually relevant ways, some separation could be required and devaluation could result. Based on this model of social and political values, Norwich (1993) has argued that there are basic dilemmas in education and in particular the field of educating students with disabilities and difficulties. These dilemmas are found in 1. the identification of students as having some distinctive kind of characteristics or needs, such as special educational needs, 2. a common curriculum for all including students with significant disabilities and difficulties and 3. the organization of education services into common schools and classes for all or specialized to some students. Clark, Dyson and Millward (1995, 1997 and 1998) have also found it useful to consider policy and practice in this field in terms of dilemmas in very similar terms.

These dilemmas of difference arise from trying to match the full range of individual needs into a common system, and need to be seen alongside further dilemmas about choice and inclusion. When facing these dilemmas individuals and agencies, whether Government and its educational agencies, local authorities or schools, either adopt established ways of resolving the tensions or construct their own strategies. There are certain established ways of finding some compatibility between these values and ideals, in which resources of finance, staffing, facilities, equipment and human capabilities all play a significant part. But, unlike other perspectives on the education of students with disabilities and difficulties, this *dilemmatic model* does not assume that tensions can be dissolved. Under changed social and economic circumstances it might be possible to reduce their sting, an experience which can nurture the hope that they will in time dissolve. What is presented, therefore, is a model of education that involves interactions within and between multiple levels (from macro to individual levels). Decisions and actions at these levels are best understood in terms of the resolution of multiple and potentially incompatible values and goals. Policy development and realization will therefore seek the optimal realization of multiple values and goals. This will depend on an acceptance that a full realization of values and principles calls for balancing and prioritizing which itself requires being at ease with a degree of ideological impurity (Norwich, 1996).

This perspective differs from others which are critical of special education from the perspective of single ideals and principles. This difference can be understood by examining a particular instance. Ainscow (1995), for example, in approaching the field is critical of the individual deficit focus and the lack of interest in systemic accommodation and response to diversity. Drawing on the work of others, especially Skrtic (1991), he uses the notion of organizational problem solving as the way to develop new responses to student diversity. Practitioners' problems are taken in his view to be soluble, if only teachers are enabled to collaborate in a problem-solving mode and if they can escape their preconceptions through critical reflections.

> I have come to the view that progress towards the creation of schools that can foster the learning of all children will only occur where teachers become more reflective and critical practitioners, capable of and empowered to investigate aspects of their practice with a view to making improvements. Only in this way can they overcome the limitations and dangers of deficit thinking, only in this way can we be sure that pupils who experience difficulties in learning can be treated with respect and viewed as potentially active and capable learners. (Ainscow, 1998:12)

If only it were so straightforward. This response is expressed by Linguard (1996), an ex-SEN coordinator who probably represents the thinking of many directly and practically involved in the field, when he argues that Ainscow s position is: 'as realistic and helpful as arguing that all teachers could become millionaires if only they were to get together and work out ways of doing it' (Linguard, 1996:40).

Clark, Dyson and Millward (1998) express similar doubts about practitioner research and theorizing, as advocated by Ainscow. To examine their teaching as a basis for improving it, they need to accumulate relevant pedagogical knowledge, which is not possible if general categories of difference and difficulties in learning are not accepted. Trying to accumulate relevant knowledge is also not open to those who criticize the project as positivist and technicist. Linguard is openly critical of 'eloquent, but impractical and utopian' statements which he considers to inhibit rather than encourage effective innovation. Clark, Dyson and Millward (1998) take a similar but less overtly critical and more moderated position, by asking rhetorically whether such approaches become 'too unproblematically and unidimensionally millennialist'. Gerber (1996:159), from his US perspective, echoes a similar concern about 'these radical proposals as misguided zealotry'. From his analysis, the demand to define educational opportunity for all disabled students in terms of location is seriously misguided: 'It is therefore unfortunate that contemporary reformers who urge "inclusion" have emphasised place over instructional substance and confused "participation" with real opportunity.' (p.158).

MODELS OF INCLUSION

None of the above arguments denies the continuing benefits of critiques of concepts and practices of separate special education and mainstream placements that ignore attempts to meet the full practical implications of inclusive ideals. These critical perspectives offer essential ways of exploring and revealing shortcomings in the system from inclusive ideals. But the critical mode is not enough and the risks are that commentators can get stuck into the deconstructive mode, finding no time nor inclination to address detailed and constructive practical approaches to policy and practice. For example, Slee (1996) refers critically to certain particular inclusion policies as attempts to combine the incompatible discourses of social justice with deficit models. He then writes that it is unsurprising that such policy represents 'attempts to manage contests and orchestrate compromises' (p.105). Slee is showing an unease with balancing and resolving tensions, which he portrays in negative terms. His concern seems to be that inclusion should not be about allocating further resources for students with disabilities, but about a 'challenge to the structure and culture of schooling' (p.105). By contrast, the position taken in this paper is that inclusion is neither exclusively about additional resourcing or different systems, nor only about challenging current schooling. Too much focus on challenge assumes that there are certainties about what is wrong and therefore what needs to be done. This is contrary to the position that there are multiple values and basic uncertainties about resolving value incompatibilities. Too much focus on additional resourcing schemes can close off some of their negative aspects and restrict vision about the goals being sought. But educating pupils with disabilities is not only about inclusion. Inclusion can be justified as both an educational means, if it enhances access and opportunities for learning, and as a goal, through learning to collaborate with others and enhancing a sense of belonging and self-respect. But it is not the only value in education and does not always promote opportunities for learning.

We will now consider several schematic models of inclusion in order to illustrate the kinds of differences we can expect from different ways of balancing the values of participating in mainstream schooling (inclusion), promoting individually relevant learning (individuality) and active involvement and empowerment (choice). As Figure 1 shows, it is useful to consider inclusion at four levels in the system: national, LEA, school and classroom levels. What is involved in inclusion is whether provision for those with difficulties and disabilities at each of these levels is built into general coverage for all or additional and different to the general coverage, what is usually called the mainstream. Whether provision is built into general coverage or is distinct can differ between these system levels. They may be distinct at one level, say in terms of national legislation with distinct provisions relating to disabilities and learning difficulties, but be part of general coverage for all at the school and classroom levels.

FIGURE 1: LEVELS OF THE SYSTEM AT WHICH PROVISION CAN BE DISTINCT OR INCLUDED IN GENERAL COVERAGE

Levels in system	provision: distinct or included in general coverage relating to:
1. National	• legislation, Government agencies, assessment curriulum, inspection and training systems
2. LEA	• policies, special and additionally resourced mainstream schools, LEA based support services
3. School	• policy and practice, staffing, learning support base for withdrawal/additional teaching
4. Classroom	• learning support, grouping and individual teaching practices

Certain key aspects of provision can be identified at each level. For national legislation and systems, this is whether legislation covering the needs of students with disabilities is additional to general coverage or considered to be included in general coverage for the full diversity of children. It is whether there are special parts to the differentiation of the national curriculum or no special differentiation for the disabled. For LEAs, this is whether there are distinct forms of organization of provision: any special schools, additionally SEN resourced mainstream schools, and external SEN support services, or just mainstream schools adapted for diversity and support services for all, not just those with disabilities. For schools, this is about distinct forms of class grouping and support for disability additional to the internal organization. For classrooms, about distinct forms of pupil grouping, support and teaching for those with disabilities and difficulties or arrangements designed to include the full diversity. Having set out a system for considering inclusion at different levels, we can now identify four models of inclusion as idealized though non-definitive schematic models which illustrate some of the key differences between different ways of balancing inclusiveness and differentiation-individualization. The first version, *full non-exclusionary inclusion,* involves the full diversity without additional or different systems at any of the four levels in the system. There would be an unconditional duty to include in neighbourhood mainstream schools and classes. Adaptive responses to diversity would be solely located at classroom level with variations in grouping and teaching being without additional, different or special systems, curricula or staffing. In this version, 'special' defined as provision that is additional or different for an identified minority is dissolved as the general provision is reformed to be adaptive to the full diversity at all levels.

In the second version, *focus on participating in the same place,* inclusion is seen to depend on the acceptance of some additional and different systems to support participation in mainstream schools and classes. This would require special legislation protecting the needs of students with disabilities and difficulties. Inclusion might be confined to some schools that are additionally resourced for the needs of the full diversity. In this version 'special' is about supporting participation in the mainstream, not what is apart from it. Therefore, there would be no separate special schools, classes or resource bases. This version shares with the full non-exclusionary model a commitment to participation in mainstream settings. It differs in accepting that to achieve this there needs to be special support systems for those with disabilities and difficulties.

Version 3, *focus on individual needs,* is committed to the greatest degree of participation in the mainstream that is compatible with meeting individual needs. The key decision-making criterion in this version is individual needs, not place as in the two previous versions. The limited use of separate settings, systems and groupings would be accepted following this criterion. But the use of special settings would depend on continuing connections between mainstream and separate settings. Limited period and part-time placements would be used as far as possible. Limited separate provision would be justified if special programmes and settings promoted longer term inclusion.

Version 4, *choice-limited inclusion*, goes even further down the route of justifying separate provision while maintaining rights to participation in mainstream schools and classes. The limit of inclusion would be in the operation of parental choice of separate programmes and settings. Parents would have their preference for mainstream or special class or school provision respected as far as possible, thus setting a limit to the inclusion of all children into mainstream settings. Though mainstream schools may be equipped to provide for the full diversity of children, this version implies limits set by individual parents, even when

FIGURE 2: DIFFERENT MODELS OF INCLUSION AND THEIR RISKS

MODELS	RISKS
1. **Full non-exclusionary inclusion** • no distinct systems	• over-prescriptive system • restriction on parental choice • individual needs of some not met • impractical
2. **Participation in the same place** • distinct support systems only	• over-prescriptive system • restriction on parental choice • individual needs of minority not met • impractical
3. **Focus on individual need** • distinct systems when necessary	• some restriction on parental choice • restricted social experiences in distinct settings
4. **Choice limited inclusion** • parental choice sets limits on inclusion	• extra need for costly resources • restricted social experiences in distinct settings • stigma for those in distinct systems

professionals or educational authorities favour the benefits of mainstream provision. The balance of power in decision making would be more to the parental than professional conceptions of individual child need.

Figure 2 sets out the four models and some of their respective risks. The full non-exclusionary inclusion model raises serious problems of principle and practice as it would involve prescriptive national legislation that could be opposed on democratic grounds of restricting parental choice. Not only would there be some doubts about enforcement, but there could be problems over meeting diverse needs without distinct support and grouping practices. By contrast, the participation in the same place model deploys distinct support systems, but there would still be doubts about restricting parental choice over the use of distinct settings. Individual needs of some with the most severe and complex disabilities might also not be met even with support in mainstream settings. The third model, focus on individual need, might involve some restriction on parental choice but far less than in the previous models. However, by using distinct settings and programmes it might restrict children's social experiences and lead them to experience stigma. By contrast, the fourth model, choice limited inclusion, requires the operation of distinct and mainstream versions of provision so that parents can choose. This could lead to additional costly resourcing. Parental choice of distinct settings could also restrict children's social experiences and lead them to experience stigma, as in the previous model.

The kind of separate provisions which follow from the last two versions are usually justified in terms of the severity of pupils' difficulties. This is either because they are thought to need to learn how to circumvent difficulties, for instance, by learning braille or sign systems, or by learning to overcome and reduce the difficulties, such as in learning of cognitive or self-control strategies. There is scope for continuing debate about appropriate goals for these pupils, whether and to what extent programmes should be distinct to focus on and recognize difficulties or whether there should be common programmes which are adapted to their individual needs. Of course, separate programmes and settings have historically also been shown to benefit the mainstream by removing students who were difficult-to-teach unless they are directly harming the education of others. But, that has not been and cannot be a legitimate reasons for separate settings. This places the onus on demonstrating the benefits of programmes focussed on difficulties, where empirical evidence plays a key role, but where there is little available.

These four models of inclusion illustrate some different balances between inclusiveness, individual need and choice. The *full non-exclusionary inclusion* version is the one where inclusiveness is predominant and where ideological purity can come to collide with democratic choice and individual need. The other *choice limited* model can from the other end perpetuate unsubstantiated claims for the efficacy of specialist settings and programmes. It can collide with the individuals' need for mainstream opportunities and social acceptance. In their pure versions, these models contradict each other. In practice, the current legislation which derives from the 1981 Education Act following the Warnock Report, embodies the model of *focusing on individual*. Parent wishes are taken into account but parents can only state a preference for special provision in mainstream settings. Education authorities are not required to comply with this preference. Under the new moves towards inclusion, this Government's commitment is towards 'promoting inclusion where parents want it' (DfEE, 1998:23). This expresses the model of *choice limited inclusion*. Within this and the *focus on individual needs* model there is plenty of scope for movement to increasing inclusion in mainstream schools. This is consistent with the second model, *participation in the same place*, but not in its pure form as this model does not accept any distinct settings, only distinct support systems. So, the currently dominant models of *choice limited inclusion* and *focus on individual need*, can coexist with *participation in the same place*, but not in its pure form. If this is true for this model, it is even more so for the *full non-exclusionary inclusion* model. So, what this analysis indicates is that so long as we recognize the multiple values that operate within education, the need to combine and balance them leads us to avoid pure choice or inclusive models. It also points to the benefits and necessity of working with multiple models and adapting them to combine with each other.

CONCLUDING COMMENTS

We have not dealt with the research reviews of inclusion in this section for two reasons. Firstly, there are several recent and not so recent reviews which indicate that there is no definitive position which arises from the empirical research (Crowther et al., 1998; Danby and Cullen, 1988; Farrell, 1997; Sebba and Sachdev, 1997).

Reviews of empirical studies have found the absence of large differences in outcomes. For example, this is the conclusion of a recent review of the outcomes for pupils with moderate learning difficulties by Crowther et al. (1998). This can be interpreted as showing that it is not the setting so much as the specific quality of provision made in a setting that is significant for learning outcomes. The effect of this kind of complexity can leave it open to proponents of separate or mainstream settings to continue their advocacy without reference to systematic empirical evidence. This is an important point as it has been commented that in an issue like inclusion there is a tendency to advocate without empirical evidence (Farrell, 1997). This tendency towards sound bites and rhetoric rather than basing judgements on a sound research base has also been commented on in the USA (Hallahan, 1998).

Secondly, it is not sensible to generalize about something like inclusion without taking account of the full range of children with significant difficulties and disabilities. Where a case study or even a large-scale survey shows what is feasible in certain contexts and areas of disability, it does not follow that generalizations can be made to other areas.

Most studies conclude that there are severe methodological limitations both in principle and practice. In principle there are ethical issues about running random allocation experiments, for example. In practice, there are problems of matching similar groups in different provision and such research is expensive to conduct. There are also issues about the range of different groups within the broad SEN field, which makes generalizing difficult. This is a critical point as there can be a tendency to generalize about the outcomes of inclusion for one group of pupils to other groups with different difficulties in learning. Similarly, there are issues in generalizing from one exemplar of inclusion to another as provision for pupils with difficulties and disabilities in mainstream settings can differ considerably. The challenge is compounded by the use of different terminology about pupils' learning characteristics and about kinds of provision across studies and from different countries.

Despite these methodological matters there is a considerable amount of empirically based literature relating to different aspects of inclusion. These take several forms – descriptive accounts by participants in professional publications, detailed case studies examining the context, developments, processes and outcomes of specific schemes, comparative or longitudinal studies of outcomes and also attitude surveys of those involved or having a stake in inclusion. Case studies have been a prominent form of evaluation recently (Alderson, 1999; Thomas et al, 1997) with systematic large-scale longitudinal studies very rare, especially in this country.

There have also been relatively few studies of the inclusion of pupils with severe and profound learning difficulties, the minority with more significant learning difficulties (Jenkinson, 1993, Farrell, 1997). The question of whether there are limits to full inclusion in the sense discussed in this chapter is best tested in relation to this group of pupils.

Farrell (1997) in his review summarizes the research evidence: most studies show the acceptability of pupils with disabilities by mainstream pupils, but that this is more common among younger pupils. For inclusion to be successful there needs to be commitment from those involved and training and support play a critical role. Some mainstream teachers are negative about inclusion, especially with pupils with more severe difficulties in learning. The importance of structured, planned and differentiated teaching programmes are underlined by the research evidence, according to Farrell. Also significant is the finding of limited and relatively didactic social and linguistic interactions between pupils with and without learning difficulties. The evidence indicates the critical role of support staff and their training, but shows that they experience a tension between devoting time to individual structured programmes and fostering social interactions. The more focus there is on the one, the less on the other, as individual teaching separates the child from others. Fostering social interaction cannot be too directive, if it is not to undermine its 'naturalness'. This tension places class and support staff in a dilemma about how much attention they give to individuals with difficulties and disabilities. The dilemma becomes more acute with pupils with more significant difficulties in learning. These teaching dilemmas can be seen to reflect the set of dilemmas of difference discussed earlier in this Section. It is the incompatibility of following contrary courses of action at different levels of the system which require some balancing and trade-offs that sets some limits to inclusion in principle. What these limits are in practice depend on multiple factors. In some favourable conditions of resourcing, commitment, adaptable and flexible mainstream schooling these limits might be slight or even negligible. In less favourable conditions the limits to inclusion may be more pronounced and involve less than ideal balances between contrary principles.

It is interesting that Farrell (1997) based on his research review sets out three models or options for long-term educational provision for pupils with significant learning difficulties. In the first – *neighbourhood inclusion* – all pupils go to their local school where resources and support would be available. This is similar to the two models discussed above – *full non-exclusive inclusion* and *participation in the same place.* Though this model can work for some areas of difficulties and disabilities and for younger children, Farrell's weighing of the case for and against this model comes down against it for pupils with more significant learning difficulties. The critical points are: 1. increasing attainment gaps lead to greater differentiation of teaching and consequently more separation in the mainstream; 2. increasing difficulties of fostering social interaction with older and more disabled pupils; 3. increased cost if adequate resourcing and support is provided. Farrell's second option is *special school with outreach* which is seen as a less radical form of inclusion. What detracts from it, according to his analysis, is not only this, but also that it can become expensive if two systems are operated, one in the special school and the other in the mainstream. His third and preferred option is *units in mainstream schools.* In this model which has been adopted in some areas, the whole population of a special school would be relocated into a group of mainstream schools, say, three primaries, a secondary and a further education college. This relocation would include pupils, staff, assistants and facilities to form what is called unit provision. Savings from the closing of the special school would make funds available for more favourable staffing and equipment. In Farrell's model, a head teacher of the dispersed units would be responsible for all the transferred pupils and for the staff and their support and development. This might be seen to be unnecessarily separatist. An alternative but similar kind of model based around a cluster of mainstream schools (Norwich, 1999), envisages a cluster management group which includes senior representatives from the mainstream, the specialist teachers and the LEA.

5
Do schools with more pupils with SEN have lower attainment levels in the league tables?

'This school dispels the myth that as more pupils with SEN enter mainstream schools the exam results suffer.'
(SENCO from an additionally resourced mainstream school)

INTRODUCTION

In this section we examine this question in the context of the increased competition between schools and the constraints that this places on schools being 'good' with pupils with disabilities and difficulties. As a recent study of four secondary schools which were chosen for being committed to inclusive values and practices showed, being 'good' with SEN pupils came to be seen as a double-edged sword, as it made the schools less attractive in the market place (Clarke et al, 1999). We use data from the 1998 GCSE league tables for all secondary schools in England to examine the relationship between the proportion of pupils with SEN and the school's 1998 GCSE performance. In examining the 'raw' GCSE performance indicators for schools we are aware that this does not take account of the 'value added' by schools, but that would require a value-added analysis for which data is unavailable nationally. The value-added exercise conducted by the DfEE on the 1998 GCSE results has involved a sample of about 200 schools, but there have been technical criticisms of this exercise and it does not extend to the whole country. The purpose of this analysis of data is not to evaluate schools but to find out the extent to which mainstream secondary schools can be high in the GCSE league tables and have a high proportion of SEN pupils on roll. Or is it the case that mainstream schools with higher proportions of pupils with SEN have lower exam results as registered in league tables?

SAMPLE OF SCHOOLS

The DfEE provides data on the 4,293 secondary schools for which GCSE data was collected following the 1998 GCSE examinations. From these 1,142 schools were excluded from the analysis as they were independent schools or special schools, leaving 3,151 schools which were designated as follows by the DfEE.

School type	Frequency	Percentage
Voluntary aided	318	10.1
LEA maintained	2044	64.9
Grant Maintained	646	20.5
City Technology College	15	0.5
Special Agreement	31	1.0
Voluntary controlled	97	3.1
Total	3151	

DATA USED IN ANALYSIS

DfEE provide data on several school aggregate performance indicators for each school. These include the percentage of pupils attaining 5 A-C grades or more, 5 A-G grades or more and GCSE average point scores. The latter performance indicator was used in this analysis as it takes account of each 15-year-old's GCSE performance through a points system which counts all grades from A* (8 points) to G (1 point). This indicator also correlates very highly with the other commonly quoted indicator, 5 A-C grades (correlation is 0.96).

The DfEE provide two school aggregate SEN indicators, these cover all children in the school with Statements of SEN and the numbers on stages 1 to 3 of the SEN Code of Practice. From these two indicators and using the total number of pupils on roll, it is possible to calculate three indicators:

1. percentage of pupils in school with Statement of SEN
2. percentage of pupils in school at stages 1-3 of SEN Code of Practice
3. percentage of all pupils in school designated as having SEN (stages 1-3 and statements).

There can be more confidence in the validity of the GCSE performance indicators to make comparisons between schools as there is moderation of the GCSE grades and there are relatively few different examination boards. However, with the SEN indicators there are wide variations in how schools decide whether to allocate a pupil to stage 1, 2 or 3. The SEN Code of Practice has broad guidelines for this but no criteria. By contrast, there are some general guidelines in the Code of Practice about the criteria for issuing a Statement, but these are also open to LEA interpretation and there are known to be wide variations between them in Statementing policy. This means that the stage 1-3 SEN indicator is a less valid indicator of less significant SEN than Statements are of more significant SEN. This feature of SEN data needs to be borne in mind in interpreting the results of the analysis.

RELATIONSHIP BETWEEN SCHOOL GCSE AND SEN INDICATORS

TABLE 1:   PERCENTAGE OF PUPILS WITH SEN (MEANS AND STANDARD DEVIATIONS) IN EACH OF THE TEN GCSE PERFORMANCE LEVEL GROUPS

Decile Groups	Mean % pupils at stages 1-3	Standard Deviation % pupils at stages 1-3	Mean % pupils with Statements	Standard Deviation % pupils with Statements	Mean % total pupils with SEN	Standard Deviation % pupils with SEN
1 (lowest)	29.1	13.9	3.9	2.5	33.0	14.4
2	21.6	11.3	3.8	3.2	25.7	11.8
3	20.1	9.9	3.3	2.1	23.4	10.2
4	18.4	9.1	2.9	1.8	21.3	9.3
5	16.0	7.7	2.7	1.7	18.7	8.0
6	14.2	7.0	2.6	1.5	16.8	7.3
7	13.3	6.0	2.5	1.5	15.9	6.3
8	12.8	6.2	2.2	1.4	15.0	6.5
9	11.7	5.3	1.8	1.2	13.5	5.6
10 (highest)	6.3	5.5	0.9	0.9	8.2	6.1
ANOVA	$F=161.7$, df=9,3117 P<0.0001		$F=63.5$, df=9, 3061 P<0.001		$F=172.2$, df=9,3051 P<0.001	
Total	16.4	10.5	2.7	2.1	19.4	11.1

The selected schools were divided into 10 groups according to their relative GCSE performance using the schools' average point scores. Analysis of the variation in the percentage of SEN pupils was then conducted in terms of these decile groups. Table 1 above shows the mean percentage of SEN pupils in each decile group. These data are also represented in the bar charts in the Figure below.

FIGURE 3: PERCENTAGE OF PUPILS WITH SEN IN SCHOOLS IN LOWEST TO TOP 10
PER CENT OF GCSE PERFORMANCE

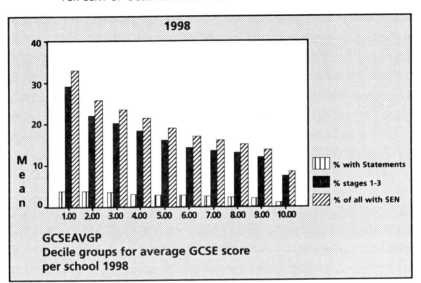

The analysis shows that in these 3,151 mainstream secondary schools there are 16.4 per cent of pupils at SEN Code stages 1-3, 2.7 per cent with Statements and 19.4 per cent with SEN overall. The difference in percentage of pupils with SEN varies across the ten performance groups in a linear way, such that as schools become higher GCSE attainers they have lower percentages of pupils with SEN for each of the three SEN indicators. The statistical significance of these differences between the decile groups were analysed using analysis of variance and shown to be highly significant.

An alternative way of representing the relationship between GCSE performance scores and percentages of pupils with SEN is through the correlation coefficients between these variables. The coefficients were as follows: -0.40 for percentage of pupils with statements, -0.57 for percentage of pupils at Code stages 1-3 and -0.58 for the percentage of all pupils with SEN (all significant at p<0.001). The lower correlation for percentage statements per school corresponds to the smaller variation between mean percentages between the decile groups in the Figure above.

For both SEN indicators there is also an increase in the standard deviation of the SEN indicator as the schools have lower GCSE performance levels. This suggests that schools with higher GCSE attainments in 1998 had less variation in the percentage of SEN pupils, while schools with lower attainments had more variation in the percentage of SEN pupils.

SCHOOLS WITH HIGH GCSE LEVELS AND HIGH PERCENTAGES OF PUPILS WITH SEN

Given the tendency for low GCSE attaining schools to have high percentages of pupils with SEN, we decided to identify those secondary schools which did not fit this pattern. In other words, we identified schools which managed to have high GCSE attainments and have high percentages of SEN. To do this, we focussed on the two base SEN indicators, pupils at Code stage 1-3 and those with statements. We adopted three levels of cut-offs for identifying schools for both GCSE and SEN indicators, the top 10 per cent, the top 20 per cent and the top 30 per cent.

The low number of schools nationally which manage to combine high GCSE performance in 1998 and high proportions of pupils with SEN can be seen by comparing Table 2 with the equivalent data in Table 3 of the number of schools with high GCSE performance and low SEN percentages. The percentage of schools which have high GCSE scores while having high percentages of pupils with SEN increases as the definition of high widens, but for neither SEN indicator does this go above 10 per cent of the high attainment group. By comparison, over

40 per cent of schools in the high attaining GCSE group had the lowest percentages of pupils with SEN.

TABLE 2: NUMBER OF SCHOOLS WITH HIGH GCSE INDICATORS AND SEN PERCENTAGES

GCSE decile group	SEN stage 1-3 group	Number of schools	% of all schools in decile group/s
Top 10 per cent	Top 10 per cent	1	0.35 per cent
Top 20 per cent	Top 20 per cent	12	2.01 per cent
Top 30 per cent	Top 30 per cent	78	8.56 per cent

GCSE decile group	SEN statement decile group	Number of schools	% of all schools in decile group/s
Top 10 per cent	Top 10 per cent	0	0
Top 20 per cent	Top 20 per cent	19	3.10 per cent
Top 30 per cent	Top 30 per cent	94	10.25 per cent

TABLE 3: NUMBER OF SCHOOLS WITH HIGH GCSE INDICATORS AND LOW SEN PERCENTAGES

GCSE decile group	SEN stage 1-3 group	Number of schools	% of all schools in decile group
Top 10 per cent	Lowest 10 per cent	153	49.20 per cent
Top 20 per cent	Lowest 20 per cent	279	44.78 per cent
Top 30 per cent	Lowest 30 per cent	495	53.00 per cent

GCSE decile group	SEN statement decile group	Number of schools	% of all schools in decile group
Top 10 per cent	Lowest 10 per cent	124	40.52 per cent
Top 20 per cent	Lowest 20 per cent	254	41.44 per cent
Top 30 per cent	Lowest 30 per cent	453	49.29 per cent

Characteristics of schools combining high GCSE levels with high percentages of pupils with SEN

For this analysis the broader criteria of high performing schools and high SEN percentages was used, that is, the top 30 per cent for GCSE and SEN data. The DfEE data enables analysis of whether these schools differ from the rest of the schools nationally in terms of their gender designation, type of school and their LEA. As regards gender designation, Tables 4 and 5 show the breakdown for those schools which are designated boys only, girls only and mixed for the two SEN indicators.

For the 78 schools identified as having high GCSE performances and high percentages of SEN (stage 1-3), a higher proportion were girls' only (12.8 v 6.6 per cent), while a lower proportion were boys only (3.8 v 5.8 per cent) or mixed schools (83.3 v 87.7 per cent). However, this was not statistically significant at the $p < 0.05$ level. For the schools identified as having high GCSE performances and high percentages with statements, a lower proportion were girls only (1.1 v 6.8 per cent) and boys only (1.1 v 5.5 per cent), while a higher proportion were mixed schools (97.9 v 88.2 per cent). This difference was significant.

TABLE 4: GENDER DESIGNATION BREAKDOWN OF IDENTIFIED SCHOOLS FOR PUPILS AT SEN CODE STAGES 1-3 (COLUMN % IN EACH CELL)

	Identified schools	Rest of schools	Totals
Girls only	10 12.8%	200 6.6%	210
Boys only	3 3.8%	176 5.8%	179
Mixed	65 83.3%	2674 87.7%	2739
Totals	78	3050	3128

(Chi-squared= 5.1, df=2, P=0.08; missing data n=23)

TABLE 5:   GENDER DESIGNATION BREAKDOWN OF IDENTIFIED SCHOOLS FOR
PUPILS WITH STATEMENTS (COLUMN % IN EACH CELL)

	Identified schools	Rest of schools	Totals
Girls only	1 1.1%	187 6.3%	188
Boys only	1 1.1%	164 5.5%	165
Mixed	92 97.9%	2632 88.2%	2724
Totals	94	2983	3077

(Chi-squared=8.3, df=2, p<0.02 ; missing data, n=74)

Tables 6 and 7 show the breakdown of the different types of schools for
the identified schools. For neither SEN indicator was there any
significant difference between identified schools and the rest of the
schools nationally in terms of the different types of school.

TABLE 6 :   TYPE OF SCHOOL BREAKDOWN OF IDENTIFIED AND OTHER SCHOOLS FOR
PUPILS AT SEN STAGES 1-3 (COLUMN % IN EACH CELL)

	Identified schools	Rest of schools	Totals
Voluntary aided	11 14.1%	306 10.1%	317
LEA maintained	49 62.8%	1989 65.4%	2038
Grant maintained	14 17.9%	607 20.0%	621
City Technology Colleges	1 1.3%	14 0.5%	15
Special agreement	1 1.3%	30 1.0%	31
Voluntary controlled	2 2.6%	94 3.1%	96
Totals	78	3040	3118

(Chi-squared-2.7, df=5, p>0.05 ; missing data, n=33)

TABLE 7 : TYPE OF SCHOOL BREAKDOWN OF IDENTIFIED AND OTHER SCHOOLS FOR
PUPILS WITH STATEMENTS (COLUMN % IN EACH CELL)

	Identified schools	Rest of schools	Totals
Voluntary aided	10 10.6%	302 10.2%	312
LEA maintained	67 71.3%	1956 65.8%	2023
Grant maintained	15 16.0%	580 19.5%	595
City Technology Colleges	0	14 0.5%	14
Special agreement	0	31 3.0%	31
Voluntary controlled	2 2.1%	90 3.0%	92
Totals	94	2973	3067

(Chi-squared- 2.7, df=5, p>0.05 ; missing data, n=84)

Tables 8 and 9 show that there was a relationship between the identified
schools and the rest of the schools in terms of whether they had a
selective admissions policy. None of the identified schools for either
SEN indicator were schools with a selective admissions policy. The vast
majority were comprehensive schools, with one secondary modern in
an LEA which still had schools with this designation.

TABLE 8:   SELECTIVE INTAKE BREAKDOWN BY IDENTIFIED AND OTHER SCHOOLS
FOR PUPILS WITH STATEMENTS

	Selective	Comprehensive	Secondary modern	Total
Identified schools	0	93 98.9%	1 1.1%	94
Other schools	91 3.1%	2725 91.7%	157 5.3%	2973
Total	91	2818	158	3067

Chi-squared=6.5, df=2, p-<0.04 ; missing data, n=84

TABLE 9: SELECTIVE INTAKE BREAKDOWN BY IDENTIFIED AND OTHER SCHOOLS
FOR PUPILS AT STAGES 1-3

	Selective	Comprehensive	Secondary modern	Total
Identified schools	0	77 98.7%	1 1.1%	78
Other schools	133 4.4%	2750 90.5%	157 5.2%	3040
Total	133	2827	158	3118

Chi-squared=6.2, df=2, p<0.04; missing data, n=33

TABLE 10: LEAS WITH TWO OR MORE IDENTIFIED SCHOOLS WHICH COMBINE HIGH
GCSE PERFORMANCE AND HIGH PERCENTAGE OF PUPILS AT SEN CODE
STAGES 1-3

LEAs	Number of schools
Hampshire (county)	12
Barnet (outer London)	5
Dorset (county)	4
Harrow (outer London) Essex (county) Oxfordshire (county) Shropshire (county) West Sussex (county)	3
Bolton (metropolitan) Sheffield (metropolitan) Brighton (unitary) Cambridgeshire (county) Cornwall (county Hertfordshire (county) Norfolk (county) Northants (county) Somerset (county)	2

TABLE 11: LEAS WITH 2 OR MORE IDENTIFIED SCHOOLS WHICH COMBINE HIGH
GCSE PERFORMANCE AND HIGH PERCENTAGE OF PUPILS WITH
STATEMENTS

LEAs	Number of schools
Cornwall (county) Lancashire (county)	10
Shropshire (county)	8
Devon (county)	7
Norfolk (county) Suffolk (county)	5
Derbyshire (county) Cambridgeshire (county) Cumbria (county)	3
Solihull (metropolitan) Doncaster (metropolitan) North Yorkshire (county) Luton (unitary) Cheshire (county) Herefordshire (county) Gloucestershire (county) Hertfordshire (county) Oxfordshire (county) Somerset (county) West Sussex (county)	2

It is clear from Tables 12 and 13 that for both the high GCSE performing
and high percentage SEN schools, using both indicators of SEN, schools
in county LEAs are in the majority. This tendency is more pronounced
for the statement indicator of SEN with almost four in five of the
identified schools being in county LEAs. Tables 10 and 11 show how
these schools are clustered in a few mainly county LEAs. For high GCSE
performing schools with high percentages of stage 1-3 pupils, there were
eight LEAs which had more than three identified schools – two were

outer London LEAs and six were county LEAs. These schools represented 46.2 per cent of all identified schools. For high GCSE performing schools with high percentages of pupils with statements, there were nine LEAs, all of which were county LEAs. These schools represented 52.2 per cent of all identified schools.

TABLE 12: BREAKDOWN OF ALL IDENTIFIED SCHOOLS BY TYPE OF LEA FOR PERCENT OF PUPILS STAGE 1-3

	Number	% of 78
Inner London	4	5.1
Outer London	17	21.8
Metropolitan	8	10.3
County	45	57.7
Unitary	4	5.1

TABLE 13: BREAKDOWN OF ALL IDENTIFIED SCHOOLS BY TYPE OF LEA FOR PERCENT OF PUPILS WITH STATEMENTS

	Number	% of 94
Inner London	0	0
Outer London	5	5.3
Metropolitan	8	8.5
County	75	79.8
Unitary	6	6.4

DISCUSSION

This analysis of the 1998 data for secondary school GCSE performance in mainstream state schools for 1998 shows that the higher the performance of the school the lower the proportion of pupils with SEN. This applies to pupils with less significant SEN (stages 1-3 SEN Code stages), for those with statements and for the total of pupils with SEN (stages 1-3 and statements combined). Not only do the higher performing schools have less pupils with SEN, but they have less variation in the number of SEN pupils than the lower attaining schools.

The next step was to identify those schools which did not fit this general tendency. We identified very few schools which had high GCSE performance and high percentage of SEN pupils. No more than 3 per cent of the top 20 per cent of GCSE performers were schools with the top 20 per cent of SEN pupils. Even when taking the top 30 per cent of schools, the proportion did not go above 10 per cent of high performing schools. However, if we take an even broader cut-off for high performing, taking this as above the national median performance level, we found 18.7 per cent and 28.1 per cent of these schools were in the top 30 per cent of schools with SEN, using the stage 1-3 and statement indicators respectively. This suggests that although the very high performing secondary schools are not the schools with high proportions of SEN, the above median performing schools feature more amongst schools with high proportions with SEN.

The correlation analysis showed that the relationship between GCSE performance and proportions of pupils with SEN is stronger for less significant SEN (stage 1-3) than more significant SEN (statements). This might be interpreted as reflecting that lower performing schools place more pupils in stages 1-3, as this allocation is school based. As statements are issued by LEAs following a statutory assessment, these schools have less influence on the statement rates. Also, it might reflect that high performing schools might be coping schools which are willing to take on additional resourcing for pupils with more significant SEN.

There were no differences between these high performing and SEN schools and the rest of the schools in terms of whether they were LEA maintained or had some other form of governance, voluntary aided, Grant Maintained and so on. In terms of gender designation, the only significant difference was a slight tendency for the identified schools to be mixed rather than boys or girls only schools. This might reflect several unrelated factors, such as where these high-attaining girls and boys only schools are located. Alternatively, it might reflect the resourcing of pupils with statements in mixed high-performing schools. However, not surprisingly, none of the high-performing and SEN schools had selective admissions policies, by comparison with the rest of the schools, of which 3-4 per cent were selective schools.

The most interesting finding about these high-performing and SEN schools was that they were located in mainly county LEAs. When pupils with statements was the indicator of SEN, there were few London schools, and of these all were from outer London LEAs, none from inner London. When pupils at stages 1-3 was the indicator, there were more London LEA schools, but mainly from outer London. There was also a tendency for these high-performing and SEN schools to cluster in certain mainly county LEAs. However, for the stage 1-3 SEN indicator, there were also two outer London LEAs with 3 or more schools.

These findings need to be interpreted with caution as discussed above. They relate to GCSE performances for one year only. These relationships need to be examined over several years. Also, as mentioned above, the validity of the SEN indicators, especially the stage 1-3 variable, is less easy to use for cross-school comparisons as the criteria for allocation are school based. This variable also aggregates across the different Code stages and so ignores the differences between stage 1 and 3 pupil numbers. Finally, this analysis of school level data does not take account of pupil level data within each school. Ideally it would be preferable to conduct this school level analysis through a multi-level modelling procedure that includes pupil level data. However, these data are not available at a national level.

The significance of this analysis is that there have been no previous analyses at a school level of GCSE performance and proportions of pupils with more and less severe SEN. Like many other empirical analyses in educational and social research the findings might not be surprising once they have been set out. However, they are relevant to commonly asserted positions, like the quote at the start of the section, that mainstream schools can combine high academic performance and high proportions of pupils with SEN. Under the current system, this is not found to be the case overall. This is why those schools, which do combine these features, are interesting and worth further study. That these schools are mainly schools from county LEAs rather than metropolitan LEAs may reflect the view that comprehensive schools, not just in name but those with a fuller diversity of intake, are more viable outside metropolitan areas in county settings. However, the findings also show that there are many more secondary schools that have above median GCSE performances and high proportions of pupils with SEN. This might point to some balancing between high academic performances in national terms and a more diverse pupil population. These are findings which are highly relevant to the issue of whether effective schools can be inclusive ones.

6
Current government policy

INTRODUCTION

Current government policy for pupils with special educational needs is framed by the government Green Paper, 'Excellence for all children: meeting special educational needs' (DfEE 1997) and its Action Programme, 'Meeting special educational needs: a programme of action' (DfEE 1998). However, the policy needs to be seen within the context of a wider government education policy geared to raising school standards. The Green Paper was issued early in the new government in October 1997 as a consultative document; over 3,600 responses to the consultation were received, and provided some of the background for the Programme of Action issued about a year later. The policy is clearly being developed both in response to problems in meeting the range of pupils' SEN, and to the pressures experienced by schools as a result of more general changes in the education system. Over the past five years there has been a steady increase in the numbers of pupils being put forward for statutory assessment and the number of statements (DfEE, 1999). This has caused pressure on LEA and school budgets, and raised issues about the most effective and equitable means of resourcing additional needs. Since the introduction of the Tribunal in 1994, there has been a growing number of cases going to tribunal appeal (SEN Tribunal, 1998). This period has also seen an increase in the number of pupils excluded from school (Parsons and Hawlett, 1996). These problems may be seen in part as a reflection of the difficulties experienced by schools in meeting the range of pupils' needs in the context of the competitive quasi-market, the pressures of inspections and league tables, combined with limited budgets and reduced LEA support (a result, among other things, of financial delegation).

Many of these problems are a result of wider changes in the education system. These include increased consumer and parental rights, the rhetoric of choice, entitlement and competition, the emphasis on raising standards of literacy and numeracy, a growing recourse to litigation and the reduced ability of LEAs to plan and to provide in an area for which they have had responsibility since the 1981 Act. They need to be seen also in the context of changes in values in relation both to SEN and to the welfare state, and to the discourses current both nationally and internationally in the field of disability, inclusion and human rights.

THE GOVERNMENT GREEN PAPER 1997

The Green Paper was welcomed as the most far-reaching review of SEN since the Warnock report almost 20 years before, and for its appearance so early in the Labour government's term of office. It claimed to offer a 'fundamental reappraisal of the way we meet special educational needs'.

It may be seen from two perspectives, first as a means to address widely recognized problems with provision for pupils with SEN, and second, as a forward-looking document which aimed to include all children within the 'standard raising' endeavour and 'excellence for all children' through its stated commitment to inclusion.

The policy of the Green Paper was summarized in David Blunkett's foreword. It set out the following themes:

- high expectations for children with SEN;

- inclusion for children with SEN within mainstream schooling;

- wherever possible support for parents;

- shifting resources from procedures to practical support and from expensive remediation to cost-effective prevention and early intervention;

- opportunities for staff development;

- promoting partnership.

It also made specific proposals including: developing special schools as centres of excellence; reducing the number of statements; additional and early support for children with emotional and behavioural difficulties; and emphasis on practical support rather than bureaucracy. It provided targets for the term of government in a language of inclusion, collaboration and partnership.

THE PROGRAMME OF ACTION 1998

The Programme of Action was produced in response to the consultation on the Green Paper (DfEE, 1997). The Action Programme provides an 'agenda for improving standards and achievement well into the twenty-first century' (p.9), sets out specific objectives and a timetable summarizing action over the next three years, and makes resources available for initiatives which will help to achieve the objectives.

The Programme is organized in five sections, corresponding with the principles of the Green Paper: working with parents to achieve excellence for all, improving the SEN framework, developing a more inclusive education system, developing knowledge and skills, working in partnership to meet special needs.

Responses to the Green Paper suggested that the majority of parents and professionals wished to retain the main features of the existing legislative framework for SEN. However, the Action Programme seeks to improve the SEN framework by a focus on preventative work and the promotion of effective school-based support. Also to be published is guidance on criteria for making statements of SEN and LEA accountability improved by monitoring against key indicators; the effectiveness of the SEN Tribunal is to be improved. The Action Programme expresses a qualified move to further inclusion of pupils with SEN in mainstream schools, with the important provisos of 'where parents want it and appropriate support can be provided' (p.23). The vision is of 'an inclusive local education system' where 'specialist provision – often, but not always, in special schools-will continue to play a vital role' (p.23). Teacher training and development for staff forms part of the objective to develop knowledge and skills, with funds allocated to promote 'SEN training' both for teachers and learning support assistants. Twenty years ago, the Warnock Report promoted partnership with parents, and multi-professional collaboration. The Action programme aims to extend regional co-ordination of SEN provision, to enable more flexible funding between education and health authorities and to improve multi-agency working.

CURRENT TENSIONS

There are a number of fundamental tensions which were evident in the 1981 Act. It is not clear how far current government policy can help to address the problems inherent in the legislation and in practice in order to provide an effective and inclusive education system for all pupils in the next century. Problems include: definition and identification of pupils with SEN, equitable resource allocation, definition of targets and standards.

DEFINING AND IDENTIFYING PUPILS WITH SPECIAL EDUCATIONAL NEEDS

The Green Paper acknowledges that the term 'special educational needs' can be misleading (p.12). However, government policy continues to use the language of identification, labelling and categorizing a certain percentage of pupils with SEN (whether this be 3 per cent, 10 per cent or 18 per cent or more). The term SEN served the needs of the time (the 1970s and 1980s) by reconceptualizing special education provision, and by raising awareness of the existence of a wider group of pupils who were not always receiving the support needed to enable them to progress. However, within a context of 'excellence for all', and common aims for education, the treatment of a group of pupils as different poses problems.

Current policy continues the practice of identifying individuals as 'special' and in need of additional resources. There is an assumption by schools, parents and LEAs that a certain number of pupils need to be identified as different. With this system, the pressures on schools lead them to identify more pupils with SEN in order to gain access to more resources, thus providing schools with perverse incentives to identify as many pupils as possible in order to qualify for additional resources. The question has to be asked how to allocate resources to schools in a way which reflects real differences in their needs, often related to their intakes, thus targeting resources appropriately and equitably, yet which provides incentives to schools to meet the needs of the wide diversity of pupils. At the same time there is the need to protect resources for the most needy individual children, particularly in mainstream schools.

ALLOCATING RESOURCES EQUITABLY

The Green Paper proposed an enhanced role for special schools, and the Action Programme mentions them as a key aspect of specialist provision. While greater partnership between special and mainstream schools is a welcome development, this raises questions. A commitment to parental choice implies the need to maintain parallel inclusive and segregated education systems, with the cost implications. 'Inclusion is a process, not a fixed state' (Booth and Ainscow, 1998:44). Inclusion involves values and school culture; unless effectiveness is defined in terms of inclusiveness, a rhetorical commitment to inclusion may conflict with other values such as individual choice and competition, and the values of the market. Inclusive policies and practices must also address the issue of social exclusion, and the demonstrated links between SEN and social disadvantage, and the growing numbers of pupils excluded from school. Here there was an opportunity for the Green Paper to interact with the White Paper, in particular with the Education Action Zones, and the Social Exclusion Unit. Nevertheless, in practical terms, greater inclusion entails shifting resources from special to mainstream sectors, and closing or at least radically changing the role of special schools.

DEFINITION OF TARGETS AND STANDARDS

The government's general commitment to raising standards of literacy and numeracy at Key Stage two and school targets raises the general question of which pupils are to be included. Target setting will apply to special schools and will be based on current work by the Qualification and Curriculum Agency (QCA) to extend and refine NC assessment criteria for student with disabilities and difficulties. This will enable teachers to assess the attainments below level 1 and between levels 1 and 3 of the NC assessment framework.

When we turn to school target setting we find that there is a similar gap for students with disabilities and difficulties. It is clear that many pupils with disabilities and difficulties in the mainstream may not reach level 4 in literacy by the year 2002, and may therefore be excluded from the uniform national target of literacy and numeracy. From a special needs perspective, there is the risk that schools will apply their resources bring pupils who are close to level 4 up to target by 2002. This could be at the expense of those less likely to reach level 4 who could then become less important to the schools. What we might find as a result of this process of selective effort is that the majority might reach the target but the variation between the highest and lowest attainers in schools might widen. This challenges, again, definitions of effectiveness, and definitions of inclusiveness, and whether schools which are effective for the majority may also be effective for all pupils.

7
Conclusions

SUMMARIZING THE POSITION SO FAR

In this concluding section we start by summariszing the main points from the previous sections. In the first section we set the question of whether effective schools can be inclusive schools in the policy context since the Warnock Report of two decades ago. In the next two sections we examined the concepts of effectiveness and inclusiveness as applied to schools. In relation to current concepts of effective schools we noted a tendency of proponents and advocates of the effectiveness approach to avoid and even criticize the values debate in education. For some the values debate is a distraction from what is judged really to count, the focus on effective means, 'what works'. We also drew attention to how the definitions of school effectiveness assumed that a minority, those with special educational needs, will not be counted in identifying school effectiveness. Yet developments in the field have led to the view that effectiveness is multi-dimensional, as schools differ in effectiveness by curriculum subject, for different groups of pupils and over time. This is a very important point as it implies that there are no empirical grounds to talk about school effectiveness as a single continuum. It implies that effectiveness phenomena have to be carefully identified in the real world of schooling. It also means that effectiveness is a complex concept and that it needs to be considered in terms of profiles based on schools' capabilities to promote learning in different areas of learning, for different groups of students and for different time periods

We noted that some school effectiveness researchers acknowledge the need to broaden effectiveness criteria but have had difficulties in doing so. We followed others who consider that they must specify what these wider outcomes are and work out how to assess them in practice. We saw this as a question of priority and balance between values and goals, while holding onto several goals. Effectiveness depends therefore on examining the relationships between different goals and outcomes, something which requires inquiry into educational values.

Development within the effectiveness field, including an examination of differential effects for different ability or attainment groups, has still not included those in special schools or even those with significant difficulties in learning in mainstream schools. Nevertheless, some theorists in the early 1990s assumed that improving schools would have benefits for pupils with SEN. What was important then was that the focus on schools as organizations provided an alternative to within-child models of difficulties in learning. But this coming together of school effective and improvement ideas and special education interests proved to be short-term and superficial. Basic differences between school effectiveness and special education interests soon began to emerge.

In our section on concepts of inclusive schools we illustrated and analysed the different conceptions of inclusion, differences which we took to have a significant bearing on the extent and nature of educational provision for pupils with disabilities and difficulties. We pointed out the difference between various concepts of inclusion: an active pupil involvement and choice of mainstream in contrast to schools responding to and accommodating all pupils. The complexity of the inclusion concept is illustrated by this contrast between placement in restructured mainstream schools and an active and chosen participation.

We noted that the popularity of inclusion in education comes from its links with wider notions of inclusivity and social inclusion. Inclusion as a process is not only connected to exclusion, but has come to apply to wider groups beyond pupils with disabilities and difficulties. Some of those who use the language of inclusive education and adopt this stance have attempted to challenge the notion of 'special educational needs'. We recognized that it is a matter of definition and choice whether inclusive education is defined to cover the wider range of disadvantaged groups or is confined to those with disabilities. But, we argued that it is important that the distinction between the more specific disability and the broader all-encompassing meanings is not blurred and confused. Overall from our analysis in section 3 we concluded that inclusion has come to be asserted and underpinned by several rights: a right to be part of the mainstream, a right to positive evaluation and respect, and a right to individually relevant learning. We saw this as another way of illustrating the complexity of inclusion and the divergent and potentially incompatible concepts of inclusion.

At this point we began to answer the question of whether what are commonly called effective school can be inclusive ones by noting that this all depends on what counts as effective and as inclusive. In the received model of school effectiveness, effective schools are identified in terms of optimizing outcomes for the majority. This leaves out the minority with greater difficulties in learning, those known to have special educational needs. This does not mean that what optimizes for the majority could not also optimize for the minority, but there is scant evidence about this matter. We will pick up this argument later in this concluding section. What we focus on now is the move to define effective in terms of inclusive values and say that for a school to be effective it has to include the diversity of pupils. As we have explained earlier, this is a position well advocated within special education circles. But this is quite a different version of effectiveness, one based on process or intake criteria, such as widening access and participation. It is not the received model version which is based on outcomes. We also noted that calls for criteria of effectiveness in terms of celebrating and welcoming difference are critical counters that wish away dominant effectiveness conceptions, rather than relate conceptually to these models.

Another option is to define effective schooling in the dual terms of intake and outcomes. In intake terms schools would be more effective, the more open access there is to the diversity of pupils in a community. In outcome terms, schools would also be more effective the more they maximize the learning outcomes of all pupils, not just the majority. In this definition of effective schooling we are working with an effectiveness concept which is based on two complex notions which are intimately connected with value issues about the degree of inclusion and about the range of desirable learning outcomes.

However, we argued that whether one adopts a process model of effectiveness (making schools effective for all by being responsive to diversity) or a more complex dual model, just outlined, it is not possible to avoid the complexity of inclusion as a value. There are several values associated with inclusion which cannot be assumed to be mutually compatible. This calls for difficult decisions that involve balancing and trading-off between contrary values or rights. This is a situation where we are faced by dilemmas of difference about providing optimally for individual learning needs and for participation and acceptance in the mainstream.

This is a position which recognizes that educating pupils with disabilities is not only about inclusion. Inclusion can be justified as both an educational means, if it enhances access and opportunities for learning, and as a goal, through learning to collaborate with others and enhancing a sense of belonging and self-respect. But, it is not the only value in education and does not necessarily always promote opportunities for learning. It is a position in which the single focus on inclusion can emphasize place over instructional substance and confuse participation with real opportunity.

Four idealized models of inclusion were outlined to illustrate some of the key differences between different ways of balancing the values of inclusiveness and differentiation-individualization: 1. full non-exclusionary inclusion; 2. focus on participating in the same place; 3. focus on individual needs; and 4. choice-limited inclusion. These were used to show that if we recognize the multiple values that operate within education and the need to combine and balance them, this goes against pure models. Our position is one of acknowledging the benefits and necessity of working with multiple models and adapting them to combine with each other.

In section 5 we switched to an analysis of English schools' latest 1998 GCSE attainments and the proportions of pupils with more and less severe SEN. Though a value-added analysis would have been preferable, as this relates to the current notion of school effectiveness, this was not feasible. However, an analysis of schools' average GCSE scores enabled us to consider whether mainstream secondary schools can combine high academic performance and high proportions of pupils with SEN. Overall, we found that this was not the case, though there was a small number of schools which did combine these features. That these schools were mainly county schools may reflect the view that comprehensive schools, not just in name but those with a fuller diversity of intake, are more viable outside metropolitan areas in county settings. However, we also found that there were many more secondary schools that have just above median GCSE performances and high proportions of pupils with SEN. This might point to some balancing between high academic performances in national terms and a more diverse pupil population.

DOES WHAT OPTIMIZES FOR THE MAJORITY OPTIMIZE FOR THE MINORITY AND VICE VERSA?

In this paper and earlier in this section we have touched on the question of whether what is 'good' for the majority of pupils is also 'good' for the minority of exceptional pupils. Those who promoted the position in the early 1990s that effective schools would benefit all pupils made this assumption. The problem here is that it is difficult to generalize to this degree as it can be argued that it is a valid assumption in some but not other respects. It is the case that there are general principles of teaching instruction and relationships which have general applicability. For example, there are principles about according respect to pupils, as well as principles about matching learning activities to individual pupils' starting levels. Though these principles can be understood to express common needs, it does not follow that the practical realization of these principles will be done in the same way for different pupils, especially those with more severe and complex special educational needs. So it is not valid to assume that what is 'effective' for most is 'effective' for the minority at the practical level of access and opportunity to have individually relevant learning activities. There are many examples of where standard kinds of access to learning are inappropriate to the needs of those with sensory and motor difficulties and with severe and complex learning difficulties.

The reverse assumption that what is 'good' for SEN is 'good' for the majority has been a rallying call of many in SEN circles. As with the other assumption it is also difficult to generalize in this way as it is a valid assumption in some respects but not in others. Where it is valid is where there may be developments and techniques which originated in response to the needs of pupils with SEN, and that can come to find a use for the majority without SEN. It is also valid in certain teaching principles which have especial relevance to those with SEN, such as individual child-centredness, which also have applicability to pupils without SEN. But, as with the reverse assumption, the principles may be common, but their realization different for different pupils. The way in which child-centredness is realized for someone with a severe emotional difficulty may be different from the majority without such emotional difficulties. Again, as with the reverse assumption, it is not valid that access adaptations that are 'good' for the minority are 'good' for the majority. For example, most people do not need enlarged print to read nor to learn braille to have access to books as do some with disabilities of sight. Nor do most need hoists to move from one area of a class-room to another, as do some with severe motor impairments.

DO WE NEED A CONCEPT OF DISTINCT NEED TO PROVIDE FOR THE DIVERSITY OF PUPILS?

We have argued that the concept of special educational needs introduced by the Warnock Report in 1978 was useful at the time, although its definition has continued to be problematic. The relative definition of SEN and the continuum of need means that it is quite possible to designate 2 per cent, 18 per cent, 20 per cent or even more pupils as having SEN. But what does this mean? The term special educational needs seems to imply the need for specialist provision or at least some distinctive pedagogy on the one hand, and additional resources or expenditure on the other hand. It may be appropriate to return to a distinction like that between 'normative' and 'non-normative' SEN (Tomlinson, 1985). According to this, 'normative' SEN usually implies some organic handicap while non-normative SEN is a broader concept, reflecting the social origins of schools and professionals struggling to provide appropriately. It is clear, then, that some pupils, for example those with severe visual impairment have distinct needs, for curriculum access through braille. It is less clear that the 20 per cent who were given the label 'special educational needs' by the Warnock Report have different needs from the majority of pupils. By widening the definition of special educational needs, the Warnock Report succeeded in increasing the number of pupils regarded as different, and whose needs could not be met legitimately by mainstream schools without additional resources.

It is important to distinguish three issues. First, there is a small minority of pupils whose needs are highly distinctive and specialist and who require specialist provision and/or teaching in order to access the curriculum. The number of these pupils is probably less than 2 per cent, such as the 1.75 per cent of the school population identified by Pijl and Meijer (1991). It might be even less than this figure, but we can be sure that there will be continuing uncertainties about drawing the boundaries. These are the pupils who can be identified as having special educational needs. The general criterion for identification would be in terms of their educational needs requiring a degree of teaching specialization that is not easily accommodated for most of a pupil's learning experiences within mainstream class learning programmes. This is compatible with inclusion in some mainstream classes and is quite consistent with these children belonging to mainstream school communities through the use of resource bases. Second, the diversity of pupils implies a need for different pedagogies and differentiated curricula, and differential allocation of resources. Equitable allocation of resources and targeting the most needy schools and/or pupils is a challenge faced by schools, LEAs and the government, and not only by the education service. This wider group of pupils may be considered to have additional educational needs. Finally, the decision whether the mainstream school should meet the needs of 80 per cent, 85 per cent, 90 per cent, 98 per cent or 100 per cent of pupils is complex. It depends on questions of values and definitions of inclusiveness, rather than on the identification of a substantial number of pupils whose needs are to be designated special and therefore different from the needs of 'ordinary' pupils. This is not to deny that some pupils have severe and complex SEN, but to suggest that the term is more appropriately confined to those whose needs are not just 'additional' but 'special' in the sense of requiring distinctive teaching.

CONCLUDING COMMENTS

We have come to the conclusion that in the dominant conception of effectiveness, we cannot answer in the affirmative to the question of whether effective schools can be inclusive ones. We have shown that this is partly built into the definition of effectiveness as non-inclusive of the full diversity. We have also illustrated this in the analysis of 1998 GCSE results. The schools achieving the highest GCSE results were not those where we find the higher concentrations of pupils with more and less severe SEN. One could ask whether schools which focus so strongly on the 5 A-C GCSE culture are likely to be welcoming and conducive places for children with difficulties in learning? But, should not our concept of the most 'effective' or 'best' schools be broad enough for it to incorporate inclusiveness? Is inclusion not at the heart of 'good' or 'effective' education? Not so, was our conclusion. Inclusion is a very important value in education, but not the only value in education. Just as important is quality teaching that addresses individual needs. In accepting that there are multiple contrary values in education, we need to resolve dilemmas by finding optimal balances and trade-offs. We have also argued that it is too easy to slip into talking about effective and inclusive schools as if these are straightforward and identifiable characteristics of schools. Our conclusion is that it is more valid to talk about schools that are effective in relation to specific criteria, for specific groups of pupils and at a particular period of time. Similarly, schools might be inclusive in some respects and not others. Both effectiveness and inclusiveness are heavily value-laden concepts. They bring us back to basic questions about aims and values in education. We need constantly to remember this and continue to be alert to attempts to reduce questions of education and schooling merely to technical and empirical questions.

REFERENCES

Ainscow, M. (1991), 'Effective schools for all: an alternative to special in education' in M. Ainscow (ed.) *Effective schools for all*. David Fulton Publishers.

— (1995), *Education for all : making it happen*. Keynote Address. International Special Education Congress. Birmingham

— (1998), 'Would it work in theory? : arguments for practitioner research and theorising in the special needs field' in C. Clark, A. Dyson and A. Millward (eds) *Theorising special education*. Routledge.

Alderson, P. (ed) (1999), *Learning and inclusion: the Cleves School experience*. David Fulton Publishers.

Audit commission/HMI (1992), *Getting in on the act. Provision for pupils with special educational needs. The national picture*. London: HMSO.

Audit Commission (1998), *Getting in on the act. A review of progress on special educational needs*. Abingdon: Audit Commission Publications.

Bailey, J. (1998), 'Australia : inclusion through categorisation' in T. Booth and M. Ainscow (eds) *From them to us : an international study of inclusion in education*. Routledge.

Barton, L. (1997), 'Inclusive education: romantic, subversive or realistic?' *International Journal of Inclusive Education*, 1, 3, 231-242.

Booth, T. (1996), 'A perspective on inclusion from England'. *Cambridge Journal of Education*, 26, 1, 87-99.

Booth, T., Ainscow, M. and Dyson, A. (1998), 'England : inclusion in a competitive system' in T. Booth and M. Ainscow (eds) *From them to us : an international study of inclusion in education*. Routledge.

Clark, C., Dyson, A. and Millward, A. (1995), *Towards inclusive schools*. David Fulton.

— (1997), *New directions in special needs: innovations in mainstream schools*. Cassell.

— (1998), 'Theorising special education' in C. Clark, A. Dyson and A. Millward (eds) *Theorising special education*. Routledge.

Clark, C., Dyson, A., Millward, A. and Robson, S. (1999), 'Theories of inclusion, theories of schools: deconstructing and reconstructing the inclusive school'. *British Educational Research Journal*, 25, 2, 157-178.

Corbett, J. (1999), 'Inclusive education and school culture'. *International Journal of Inclusive Education*, 3, 1, 53-61.

Cowne, E. and Norwich, B. (1987), *Lessons in Partnership*. London: Institute of Education, Bedford Way Papers.

Crowther, D., Dyson, A., Millward, A. (1998), *Costs and outcomes for pupils with moderate learning difficulties in special and mainstream schools*. DfEE.

CSIE and CEN (1998), *The index of inclusive schooling – guide for school co-ordinators*. CSIE.

Danby, J. and Cullen, C. (1988), 'Integration and mainstreaming: a review of the efficacy of mainstreaming and integration for mentally handicapped pupils'. *Educational Psychology*, 8, 3, 117-195.

DES (1978), *Special Educational Needs (The Warnock Report)*. London: HMSO.

DfEE (1994), *Code of Practice on the identification and assessment of special educational needs*. HMSO.

— (1997), *Excellence for all children: meeting special educational needs*. Green Paper.

— (1998), *Meeting special educational needs : a programme of action*.

— (1999), *DfEE Statistical First Release SFR 10/1999 Special Educational Needs in England*.

Evans, J. and Lunt, I. (1994), *Markets, competition and vulnerability.* London File.

Farrell, P. (1997), *Teaching pupils with learning difficulties: strategies and solutions.* Cassell.

Fish, J. (1985), *The way ahead.* Open University Press.

Florian, L. (1998), 'Inclusive practice; what, why and how?' in C. Tilstone, L. Florian and R. Rose (eds) *Promoting inclusive practice.* Routledge.

Gerber, M. (1996), 'Reforming special education: beyond inclusion' in C. Christensen and F. Rizvi (eds) *Disability and the dilemmas of education and justice.* Open University Press.

Gipps, C., Gross, H. and Goldstein, H. (1986), *Warnock's 18 per cent.* Lewes: Falmer Press.

Goacher, B., Evans, J., Welton, J. and Wedell, K. (1988), *Policy and provision for Special Educational Needs.* London: Cassell.

Goldstein, H. and Thomas, S. (1995), 'School effectiveness and value added analysis', *Forum*, 37, 2 36-38

Goldstein, H. and Myers, K. (1997), 'School effectiveness research: a bandwagon, a hijack or a journey towards enlightenment?' Paper at British Educational Research Association, York. (http://www.ioe.ac.uk/hgoldstn/serescrit.html)

Grace, G. (1998), 'Realising the mission: catholic approaches to school effectiveness' in R. Slee, G. Weiner and S. Tomlinson (eds) *School effectiveness for whom?* Falmer Press.

Gray, J., Goldstein, H. and Jesson, D. (1996), 'Changes and improvements in schools' effectiveness: trends over five years'. *Research papers in Education*, 11, 35-51.

Guardian (1998), *A class of her own.*, 27.5.98.

Hallahan, D. P. (1998), 'Sound bites from special education reform rhetoric'. *Remedial and Special Education*, 18, 2, 67-69.

Hamilton, D. (1996), 'Peddling feel-good fictions', *Forum*, 38, 2, 54-56.

Jenkinson, J. C. (1993), 'Integration of students with severe and multiple learning difficulties'. *European Journal of Special Needs Education*, 8, 3, 320-355.

Linguard, T. (1996), 'Why our theoretical models of integration are inhibiting effective innovations'. *Emotional and Behavioural Difficulties*, 1, 2, 39-45.

Lauder, H., Jamieson, I. and Wikeley, F. (1998), 'Models of effective schools: limits and capabilities' in R. Slee, G. Weiner and S. Tomlinson (eds) *School effectiveness for whom?* Falmer Press.

Low, C. (1997), 'Is inclusivism possible?' *European Journal of Special Needs Education* 12, 1, 71-79.

Lunt, I. and Evans, J. (1994), 'Allocating resources for special educational needs provision', *Policy Options for Special Educational Needs in the 1990s.* Stafford: NASEN.

Maclure, S. (1988), *Education reformed.* London: Hodder & Stoughton.

Mortimore, P. (1995), *Effective schools: current impact and future possibilities.* The Director's Inaugural lecture. Institute of Education, University of London.

— (1998), *The road to improvement: reflections on school effectiveness.* Zwets and Zeitlinger.

Mortimore, P. and Sammons, P. (1997), 'End piece: a welcome and reposte to critics' in J. White and M. Barber *Perspectives on school effectiveness and school improvement.* Bedford Way papers. Institute of Education, University of London.

Mortimore, P., Sammons, P., Stoll, L., Lewis, D. and Ecob, R. (1988), *School Matters: the junior years.* Wells, Open Books.

Norwich, B. (1990), *Reappraising special needs education.* Cassell.

— (1992), *Time to change the 1981 Act.* London File. London: Tufnell Press.

— (1993), 'Ideological dilemmas in special needs education : practitioners' views'. *Oxford Review of Education* 19, 4, 527-546.

— (1994), 'A US-English comparison of attitudes to integration'. *European Journal of Special Needs Education,* 9, 1, 91-106.

— (1994), *Segregation and inclusion. English LEA Statistics 1988-1992.* Bristol: CSIE.

— (1996), 'Special needs education or education for all : connective specialisation and ideological impurity'. *British Journal of Special Education.* 23, 3, 100-104.

— (1997), *A trend towards inclusion.* Bristol: CSIE.

— (ed) (1998), 'Aims and principles' in *Future Policy for SEN : responding to the Green Paper.* SEN Policy Option Steering Group (Ed.) NASEN.

— (1999), 'Inclusion in education : from concepts, values and critique to practice', in *The future of special education.* Falmer Press (in press).

Oliver, M. (1992), 'Intellectual masturbation: a rejoinder to Söder and Booth'. *European Journal of Special Needs Education,* 7, 20-28.

Parsons, C. and Howlett, K. (1996), 'Permanent exclusions from school: a case where society is failing its children'. *Support for learning,* 11,3,109-112.

Pijl, S. and Meijer, C. (1991), 'Does integration, count for much? An analysis of the practices of integration in eight countries'. *European Journal of Special Needs Education,* 6(2):100-111.

Pumfrey, P. (1996), *Specific developmental dyslexia: back to basics.* Vernon-Wall Lecture, Leicester: BPS.

QCA (1998), 'Target setting for special schools', London: QCA.

Ramasut, A. and Reynolds, D. (1993), 'Developing effective whole school approaches to special educational needs: from school effectiveness to school development practice', in R. Slee (ed.) *Is there a desk with my name on it?: the politics of integration.* Falmer Press.

Reynolds, D. (1995), 'Using school effectiveness knowledge for children with special needs - problems and possibilities' in C. Clark, A. Dyson and A. Milward (eds) *Towards inclusive schools.* David Fulton.

— (1998), 'The school effectiveness mission has only just begun'. *Times Educational Supplement*, February 20.

Scott, D. (1997), 'The missing hermeneutical dimension in mathematical modelling of school effectiveness' in J. White and M. Barber (eds) *Perspectives on school effectiveness and school improvement.* Bedford Way Papers. Institute of Education, University of London.

Sebba, J. and Sachdev, D. (1997), *What works in inclusive education?* Barnados.

Skrtic, T. M. (1991), 'Students with special educational needs: artifacts of the traditional curriculum' in M. Aisncow (ed.) *Effective schools for all.* David Fulton.

Slee, R. (1996), 'Disability, class and poverty : school structures and policing identities' in C. Christensen and F. Rizvi (eds) *Disability and the dilemmas of education and justice.* Open University Press.

Slee, R. and Weiner, G. (1998), 'Introduction' in R. Slee, G. Weiner and S. Tomlinson (eds) *School effectiveness for whom?* Falmer Press.

Slee, R. (1998), 'High reliability organisations and liability students — the politics of recognition' in R. Slee, G. Weiner and S. Tomlinson (eds) *School effectiveness for whom?* Falmer Press.

Slee, R., Weiner, G. and Tomlinson, S. (eds) (1998), *School effectiveness for whom?* Falmer Press.

Special Educational Needs Tribunal (1998), *Annual report 1997-98.* DfEE.

— (1997), *Annual Report, 1996-7.* London: DfEE.

Stoll, L. (1991), 'School effectiveness in action: supporting growth in schools and classrooms' in M. Ainscow (ed.) *Effective schools for all,* David Fulton Publishers.

Stoll, L. and Mortimore, P. (1997), 'School effectiveness and school improvement' in J. White and M. Barber (eds) *Perspectives on school effectiveness and school improvement,* Bedford Way Papers, Institute of Education, University of London.

Swann, W. (1985), 'Is the integration of children with special needs happening? An analysis of recent statistics of pupils in special schools'. *Oxford Review of Education,* 11,1,3-18.

— (1988), 'Trends in special school placement to 1986: measuring, assessing and explaining segregation'. *Oxford Review of Education,* 14,2,139-161.

— (1992), *Segregation statistics English LEAs 1988-91.* London: CSIE.

Thomas, G. (1997), 'Inclusive schools for an inclusive society'. *British Journal of Special Education,* 24,3,103-107.

Thomas, G., Walker, D. and Wenn, J. (1998), *The making of the inclusive school.* Routledge.

Thomas, S., Sammons, P., Mortimore, P. and Smees, R. (1997), 'Stability and consistency in secondary schools' effects on students' GCSE outcomes over three years'. *School Effectiveness and School Improvement,* 8, 169-197.

Times Educational Supplement (1998), 'Primary targets threat to weaker pupils'. 29.5.98.

Tomlinson, J. (1997), 'Inclusive learning : the report of the Committee of Enquiry into post-school education of those with learning difficulties and disabilities in England 1996', *European Journal of Special Needs Education*, 12, 3, 184-186.

UNESCO (1994), *The Salamanca Statement and Framework on Special Needs Education*. UNESCO

Vevers, P. (1992), 'Getting in on the Act'. *British Journal of Special Education*, 19,3,88-92.

Wedell, K. (1990), 'Special education: past, present and future' in P. Evans and V. Varmer (eds) *Special Education: Past, Present and Future.* Lewes: Falmer Press.

Walzer, M. (1983), *Spheres of Justice.* Oxford: Blackwells.

White, J. (1997), 'Philosophical perspectives on school effectiveness and school improvement' in J. White and M. Barber (eds) *Perspectives on school effectiveness and school improvement.*

White, J. and Barber, M. (1997), *Perspectives on school effectiveness and school improvement.* Bedford Way Papers. Institute of Education, University of London.